AF486893

The Stock Market Way

5 Steps
Towards
Wealth

PIYUSH PATEL

notionpress
.com

INDIA · SINGAPORE · MALAYSIA

Copyright © Piyush Patel 2023
All Rights Reserved.

ISBN

Hardcase 979-8-89133-645-2
Paperback 979-8-89026-960-7

This book has been published with all efforts taken to make the material error-free after the consent of the author. However, the author and the publisher do not assume and hereby disclaim any liability to any party for any loss, damage, or disruption caused by errors or omissions, whether such errors or omissions result from negligence, accident, or any other cause.

While every effort has been made to avoid any mistake or omission, this publication is being sold on the condition and understanding that neither the author nor the publishers or printers would be liable in any manner to any person by reason of any mistake or omission in this publication or for any action taken or omitted to be taken or advice rendered or accepted on the basis of this work. For any defect in printing or binding the publishers will be liable only to replace the defective copy by another copy of this work then available.

DEDICATION

This Book is dedicated to my Family, especially Mother who was a teacher and seeds of teaching were sown by her. She instilled in me a love for reading and learning. My Father, Wife & Daughters whose unwavering support and encouragement have been my guiding light on this literary journey. Dedicated to my Profit Team who were there to take care of services when I was busy writing the book. To my Profit Family across the world for giving me unconditional Love. I should definitely say that without their support nobody would recognize us. Love To all my friends and relatives who were there always at any time. To my younger sister who is a professor and has always insisted on me for upgrading my education. To Mrs. Shaila Prabu (Bengaluru) who extracted her learnings from our different education programs and put it in writing while the creation of this book.

Table of Contents

Introduction

Why This Book?

Should I read this book? India as a country of millennials is heading towards a high jump in productivity and income. Young Indians are looking for investment ideas and strategies that are practical, easy to implement, risk-free and tension-free. While they begin the journey with high momentum, as time goes by, the momentum decreases, and the expected results are not achieved. Many young dreams have been buried with the music still on, with directionless strategies making the end results timid. What could have gone wrong? Did the flaws lie with the plan, the strategies or the implementation?

This book is not for those looking for a Quick Rich Scheme (QRS) or a strategy to become a millionaire overnight. It is for those investors who are looking to create sustainable wealth and leave a legacy that could pay them for years and years. The asset class they create over time will help them achieve their dreams and pay off all their liabilities too. Yes, this book can change the direction and accelerate the speed of their Return on Investment (ROI).

Let me introduce myself. I am Piyush Patel

- A college dropout.
- A normal, middle-class salaried person.
- I have zero knowledge about the stock market.
- I don't have a financial background. (My mother is a proud teacher and my father, a shopkeeper.)

From these humble beginnings, if I could transform my life, starting as a novice investor and eventually running India's top stock market training institute, simultaneously becoming debt free and creating assets that can take care of my dreams and liabilities, then, my dear friends, you can do it too!

During my 15 years of teaching, I have seen investors transforming their investments from mud to gold, becoming highly confident, and progressing magnificently on the road towards wealth.

Fifteen years ago, I had nothing except many books in my cupboard. No Laxmi, only Saraswathi, – with empty pockets but a mind full of energy. I was not even confident at that time that *apna time ayega*, but yes, I'm proud that Saraswathi helped me achieve Laxmi, fame and the love of investors.

Who helped me during that difficult time? Who gave me confidence despite my empty pockets? Yes, I only had books which helped me get through those challenging days. Today, I can proudly say that books are amazing! Books create the wiring in our brains that can last forever.

During those challenging days, I used to think, *Unke paas ghar hai, gadi, bangla hai. Mere paas kya hai?"* Yes, just a cupboard full of books! But those books have an amazing power to attract health, wealth, good relationships, or anything else you dream about.

I ask you today, "What do you have?" One more book in your hand! But take a pause; this book is going to pave the way to catapult your assets value for the next 30 years. Be ready, fasten your seat belts and let us fly!

Five Steps Towards Wealth

I will discuss five effective yet simple steps that anyone can take to move towards wealth. A thousand investors from varied backgrounds across the country are already succeeding by following these steps. People from all age groups and professional backgrounds have tested it and figured a way to use these simple steps.

With loads of enthusiasm to learn about the market, I would meet with some of my friends and discuss current trends, the condition of the economy, industries and sectors, stock markets, investment options, financial trends and so many other interesting topics at regular intervals. The quarterly results announcement of listed companies interested us the most.

For a long time, we used to analyze the latest results and updates of companies, adjust the current trends and expectations with recent results and discuss it. It gave us an understanding of how sectors were performing, noticing some of the hurdles they faced from time to time. When we met, we would share our learnings with each other. It kept our interest afloat and built our expertise in the field over time.

This small meeting soon became popular, and the number of attendees grew. Many people told us that the topics discussed and practised had given them insights. It helped many small investors get on track. Many of them pressed the get-set-go button on the path to wealth creation.

For a few years, these meetings were annually organized at Vadodara, Surat, Rajkot and Ahmedabad. In one such event in Rajkot, Gujarat, we decided to take this meeting to all the states in India. At that time, the name of the meeting was 'Latest Results Update Meet.' Some participants suggested that we name it 'The Five Steps to Wealth Creation' because they had clearly perceived five important steps to wealth creation from our discussions and teachings. Our purpose was to inspire the growing tribe of investors in India to be in tune with current trends and keep ourselves abreast on a regular basis. We had made it a habit to keep track of the results and performance of companies and observe their growth, their business decisions, the outcomes, etc., because we realized that each one of us should personally understand and take responsibility for the financial decisions we make, instead of following others blindly.

Most investors are not aware of the value of keeping track of company results. Results help us understand whether the company has performed well or not over the given period. Without a fair idea about the sector and company performance, most investors take rash and uninformed decisions that they regret later. It is too late when they get to know that their company has started drowning in debt or has other problems. Nor do they foresee that their company and sector are doing very good business and are going to outperform the market. So, invariably, most people end up selling too early or buying too late, i.e., at very high valuations, or they get stuck with the losers. Either way, if an investor is uninformed, he generally stands to lose in the market. He becomes easy prey to false news, tipsters and scamsters.

Often, innocent investors are trapped in hyper-trading activities too. Trading instruments like futures and options, BTST, Intraday trading, etc., are sponsored products meant only to generate brokerage, not wealth. It creates excitement at the stock terminal but not in the portfolio.

Over the years, our premier programme, 'The Five Steps to Wealth Creation,' has become very popular. It is an interactive programme and entry is still free. Today, we charge a nominal commitment fee of Rs.1 meant to rule out uncommitted participants. In the meetings, we discuss the needs and challenges of various age groups on their financial journey. Through our continuous interaction with several people across the country, it became clear that there are only a few simple things that we must do consistently to keep us on the track to wealth creation. We need to smoothly manage our financial portfolio. Yes, it might not be easy, but it is simple. Sometimes, doing simple things consistently is not easy.

This programme is almost a decade young now, and so we decided to offer it to everyone in the form of a valuable book. Books have always inspired and supported me, even when there was no information technology and backup as there is today.

The five steps discussed in detail in this book are:

1. Financial planning: Managing our hard-earned money in a better way.
2. Growing economy: Investing in the booming economy.
3. Demanding industries: Looking for demanding industries from the booming economy.
4. Top-quality companies: Searching for top-quality companies from demanding industries which can grow and give consistent income – companies that can remain viable for long.

5. Creation of a wealth portfolio of assets that can stay, grow and pay in the long run, risk free and stress free.

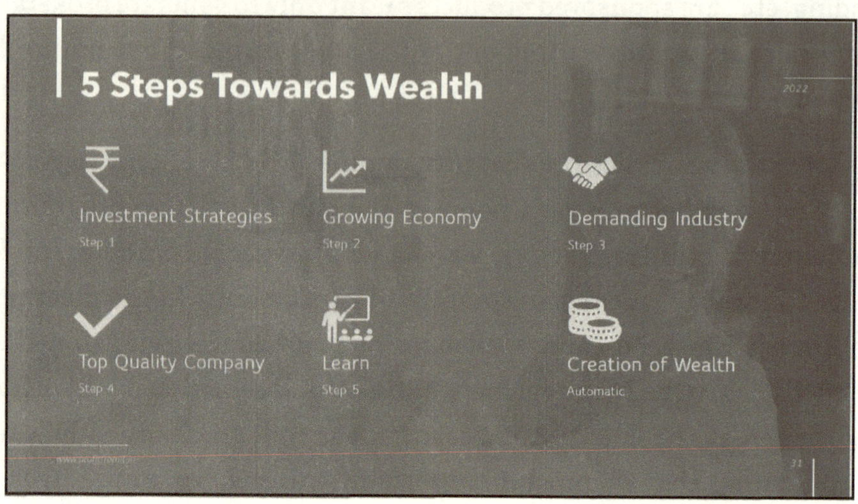

Let us begin the story with the first point: Financial planning. Are you ready? If yes, then let us take off!

STEP 1

Financial Planning: Managing Our Hard-Earned Money in a Better Way

> "In the long run, it's not just how much money you make that will determine your future prosperity. It's how much of that money you put to work by saving it and investing it."
>
> **– Peter Lynch**

What and Why?

Financial planning is a step-by-step approach to estimating the required capital and determining how to acquire the same. Simply put, it helps you keep track of your income, expenses, savings and investments so that you can manage your finances better. Money should work for you, not the other way around.

Challenges

1. How will I increase my income to achieve my goals?
2. How will I become secure so that I can feel safe and financially free?
3. How to retire young and rich?

Between 25 to 30 years is the average age an Indian starts a career after his education. Let's begin with this age group and gradually we will plan for all age groups of investors.

Career

In India, people start looking for a career around the age of 25. People start earning immediately after they complete their higher education. Many people opt to continue their education along with their professional life.

I opted to start earning at the early age of 19 and was always looking for an alternate way to make money, money and more money. My dreams were big, but my salary was small. I purchased my *dream bike* with my first salary itself, without even waiting for my second salary slip. Along with my salary, my instalments also began. Why did I not wait for my second month's salary? Because, at that time, even buying a bike was a big dream. Until then, I had been dependent, without any earnings. Suddenly, I was in seventh heaven because the money had just started coming in. My own money! The cash flow was ON. I did not know that when money starts coming in, if I didn't manage it properly, it would find its way out quickly. I was simply happy because I was able to purchase something for the first time on my own. But at the same time, I was sad too, because by the last day of the month, I had no money in my pocket.

This was the genesis of 'chasing after my dreams' with external funding, paying creditors first and myself later. What could I do? How could I increase my income for petrol and other necessities? The list of wants was too long, longer than my salary slip. I was happy with my salary, yet sad about my empty bank account.

I had just completed work and sat at the table, dejectedly picking up a book from the library. I read about the success stories of business giants who had started from zero. It inspired me in two very important ways. The first was the importance of reading books as they have the power to motivate you, giving you hope during the bad times. Secondly, I understood that one can do anything one visualizes.

It inspired me, and along with my friends, I decided to start a business, while keeping my day job. With no idea as to what business to start, but with the hope that we would achieve great things, we started multiple side businesses one after another, as we were clueless about which business would be viable – until we were successful that is. Yes! I had made a decent amount of money by the age of 21.

Again, let me tell you, my dreams were big, but my income still fell short. I needed a car. I could not afford to buy a car with my income at that point, but banks and finance companies were there to lend, and the rat race started. Yes, I got loans from banks to fulfil my dreams. The cost of early gratification of my dreams with borrowed money was high, but I did not understand that achieving my dreams with borrowed money could be expensive for me. I was happy because one more dream had been accomplished. In reality, my situation was bleak as I had no money left for petrol or some emergency at the end of the month, after paying all the instalments. EMI Mote! *Pagaar Patle!*

I considered working harder. My mother used to tell me, "*Beta,* save money." My father used to tell me to save at least 10% of what I earned. But I thought I was smarter. In Gujarati we say, *Dod-Dahyo* (over smart). I have also heard somewhere that if you don't save money, all you need to do is increase your income. I went with this motto and increased my income. My income used to increase month on month, but my liabilities held me down. Money would come into my bank account, but I made several holes in it, so the money didn't stay there long. My dreams included a car, a big house, foreign trips, and a good lifestyle, all facilitated by EMIs. But along this path, I forgot that I needed security, peace of mind, friends, good health, etc. The instalments were high, and I paid them regularly.

Around the year 2002, I was unable to manage the short-term (2 years) downturn of a muted economy. My income fell slightly, but I couldn't afford even this small decline due to the large EMIs, and I realized that I had messed up. I could survive only if my income continued to increase because I had planned for EMIs and other costs expecting my income to increase. When you achieve your dreams from resources other than your own assets, the cost is steep! I realized that I could have waited for some time and created the assets to support my dreams; then the story would have been different.

Despite my substantial income, I only created liabilities. I remember buying the Raymond suit for my wedding, which made me a 'complete man,' using my credit card. I thought to myself, *I've been working like a bull for five years, but what have I created for myself? Liabilities, stress, an irritated mind, and no assets.* The year was 2003. I wondered how to get out of this debt burden. My business was not good due to the financial crisis. I had created liabilities with zero assets and tried to become over smart even with my parents. How would I face them? As the good times had lasted for several years, the bad times also stayed for several years. I was jobless, income-less, car-less, and bike-less. However, I hoped that someday, I would stand tall again, and this time I would create the assets that would see me through the bad times. I swore that I would avoid liabilities.

I had my family and my books. When you are stuck, everything goes wrong. I could not even afford an immediate urgent operation for my daughter; it was the first time my eyes were filled with tears. I knew there was no money in my bank account. Regardless, I frequently checked my bank balance as I had already committed to the doctor. Thank God that I received help from my mother's friend for the operation. My little one survived. This was the toughest lesson I had learned. Money might not be everything, but yes, we need money to live with dignity.

I had learned several invaluable lessons during this period. During that Diwali, I recall sitting in a public place full of noise and people who were in a celebratory mood. Meanwhile, I was reeling from the consequences of a big business and family failure, left with nothing except a few books. As a black belt in Tae-Kwon-Do, I had learned that *till you are not dead, till the last breath you can intake, you can bounce back.* Failure was not an option.

I decided not to repeat the mistakes of the past. I would slowly, steadily try to recover the business and avoid creating liabilities. I would create huge assets that would take care of my dreams and ensure my security. What I needed was not just finance to pay off my debts. I needed a proper financial plan – a plan to create assets along with a stress-free life, health and security. This time, I was not in a hurry to achieve my dreams. I set goals with a realistic approach. I understood that it would take time. I would achieve my dreams with my own money.

I asked my parents and my family to give me some time and promised that we would create history. I would create huge assets in time. I would focus on the creation of assets that would see me through the bad times. I knew that in life, we had to face both the good and bad times. It's hard to foresee whether times would be good or bad. It was necessary to be always prepared for contingencies in advance.

This was a real riches-to-rags story due to badly managed finances and then I got back on track to founding India's top stock market training institute. This is not just my story; this is the story of any average individual who makes money working hard but doesn't know how to manage their finances. As the average Indian starts making money at the age of 25, they have several wants, and start purchasing things to satisfy their wants, thinking that such material things will make them happy – the more they buy, the better life will be. But the truth is, happiness comes from within.

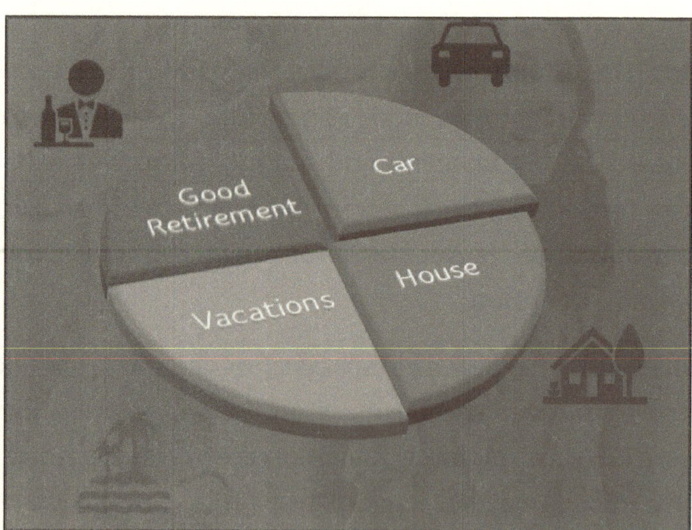

In general, people want security, but they also crave a car, a house, vacations, etc., along with the basic needs of life. Hence, they start purchasing these things on instalments, setting a trap for themselves, moving further away from financial independence. As the years pass by, our salaries increase, our dreams get bigger, our EMIs get bigger, and this trap gets larger and larger. We reach the stage where we:

1. Cannot afford to rest or go on a holiday
2. Cannot afford to retire early
3. Feel insecure and have no financial freedom

The value of life virtually disappears!

Life's Needs in General

Age Bracket	Event That Costs or Gives Money	Easy Way	Mature Way	Impact
20–25	First job or business			Happy mind
20–25	Buy a bike and/or a new car	EMI	Invest and buy a vehicle with your own money after a few years	Stress-free life
	Get married	EMI	Save money in advance	Stress-free life
26–35	Buy a home	EMI	Invest and buy a house with your own money after a few years	Stress-free life
	Child's education	EMI	Save money in advance	Stress-free life
36–50	Plan for retirement	Work even after retirement	Make investments that can pay lifelong	Stress-free life
50+	Retire	Work even after retirement	Make investments that can pay lifelong	Stress-free life

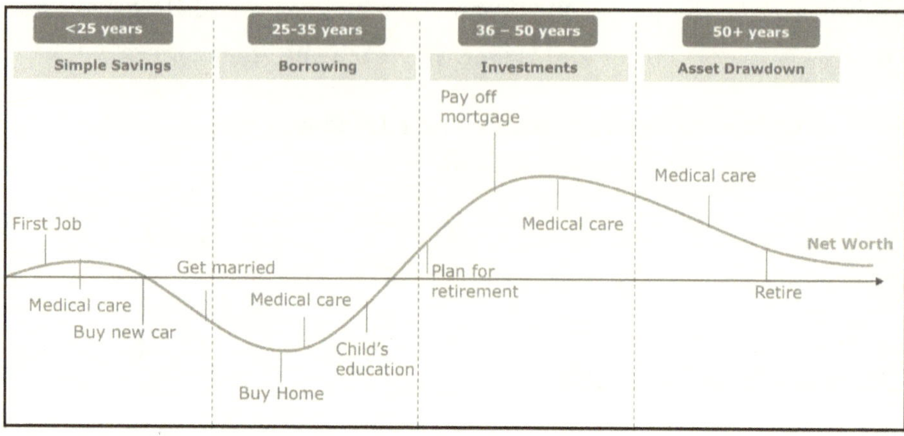

The above chart depicts the standard lifecycle of a person. Most of us have some idea about the general pattern of our lifecycle and it should help us plan for the different stages of our life in advance. But the general trend for most of us is to create more liabilities than assets due to easy credit facilities made available at the drop of a hat. While expenses and EMIs grow uncontrollably, our sources of income remain limited, and this trend totally destroys our financial planning.

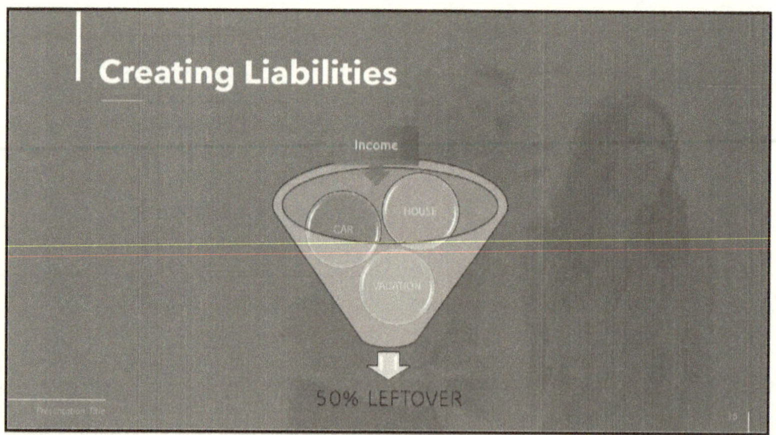

When EMIs pile up, our funds get flushed out rapidly. When this pattern continues month on month, our income doesn't stay in our account long enough to accumulate. Our account balance will never grow into significant savings, even if we work long hours our entire life! Precious years melt away in the struggle to change this picture.

So, is there a way to get out of this *Maya Jaal* of unlimited wants and needs? Is there a way to curb this impulsive spending spree?

With our first salary comes a sense of personal responsibility, but schools and colleges don't teach us the skills necessary to be financially responsible. So, we all need to learn how to create a financial plan. Planning helps us to chart out the route, as we start our journey and create that much-needed value and purpose of life.

To bring our finances back on track, we must monitor both our money and our emotions. Instead of impulsively deciding what to buy next, how about spending just a few minutes every month checking our personal finances? It's as simple as that! Without basic financial understanding, we will repeatedly face painful consequences.

Reading and researching surely encouraged me to set aside the over-smart mindset. I used to rely on clever tricks and shortcuts to solve everything. But with a *josh* to change and refreshed awareness, the search was on for a genuine and straightforward way out.

I started thinking about these puzzling questions more deeply:

- Is it better to save and slowly build assets, or is it better to use debt/credit as the main route to satisfy all my wants quickly?
- Is it possible to create assets with just one or two sources of income?
- Is there a way to differentiate a good debt from a bad one?

The answers are available. Yet, most of the time, in a mad rush to buy a car, house, or anything else we fancy on easy loan schemes, and go on vacations, the above questions are brushed aside till some emergency hits us head on.

Thanks to tough times, I learned many bitter lessons, but my passion to achieve my goals pushed me further on. The time had come to erase my past mistakes. I learned a few important things that gave me the courage to sort out difficult situations and press the **Restart and Refresh** button on my finances. On the way, I hope to inspire and guide many people to do the same and achieve their financial milestones.

So, stay with me for answers to these questions, and we will see how the slightest change in routine financial habits can help resolve many sticky issues. We just need to **Reform-Perform-Transform** on our way to a brighter future.

Where we stand as of today is the outcome of our past decisions and choices. To press the 'Enter' button on Reforms, we must change our thinking and allow new learnings, skills and discipline in our actions. Next, we must actually 'act upon it' and perform these new actions with awareness. We must have a systematic follow-up routine. Consistently reforming and performing the required actions will produce the transformation that we seek. Let me explain.

India is on the path of reform, and we have seen how big companies and corporations have faced challenges in the economy over the years. They have grown their business from small to large and today, they are big enough to compete in world markets! On a personal level also, ask yourself this question: *Where am I today? Where do I want to be in 'X' number of years from now? What resources do I currently have? What should I change? What will I have by the end of one month, a year, or a few years ahead?*

Way back then, I realized that my net worth was negative. I was heavy on debts and light on assets. I decided to change this picture and be light on debts and heavy on assets. I needed to create assets that could support and give me some cushioning. I wanted to carve out a path towards wealth creation. I needed to take charge of my random behaviour and look keenly at what I was doing with my income and expenses!

A closer look at my behaviour encouraged me to map the flow of my incoming and outgoing funds. It really helped me understand how cash flowed in and out of my pocket. It is a tool to track **where you are** currently placed because of your financial habits.

This study of your personal cash flow is a very crucial step.

Money Moves Around in Four Slots

1. Incomes
2. Expenses
3. Assets
4. Liabilities

Income is what we receive, while expense is what goes out of our pockets. Assets are what we own, and liabilities are what we owe to others. Simple, right?

Balancing the entries and exits from these four slots is essential. This is what can unfold magic! If we check our incoming and outgoing cash flow regularly, we may not make the mistake of over-spending.

1. INCOMES (+)	2. EXPENSES (-)
• Wages/salary	• Food and clothing
• Business income	• Mortgage, rent
• Rental income	• Transport
• Royalties	• Taxes and bills
• Dividends/interest	• Credit card and utilities
	• Education
	• Holidays
	• Luxuries

3. ASSETS (+)	4. LIABILITIES (-)
• Bank savings • Real estate, land, property • Business • Intellectual property • Bonds and stocks • Precious metals	• Mortgages • Consumer credits and loans • Credit card debts • Leverage

Make this simple list for yourself and see how your clarity improves. Pre-planning our outflows every month really helps. Just a little focus is needed to track the incomes, expenses, investments and outflows. This is a habit worth the effort. Having a financial strategy works wonders. Planning is of strategic importance to managing our hard-earned money in a better way.

In the chart above, we can see that there are many ways for cash to flow in. These are called earnings and incomes. Money also has ways of flowing out in the form of expenses and liabilities, EMIs, debts, etc.

We earn a salary from our job; we earn some profits from business or rental income, etc. Some of us even earn interest from past investments. We can even plan for the money to flow in regularly from dividends, rental income, etc. These are the inflows in our account. We must have a goal to create passive income from multiple sources. But even before the earnings can come in, what about the long line of expenses which are already marching ahead to gobble up the balance?

All of us incur mandatory expenses like groceries and various other bills every month. We all know that it is better to pay the bills on time, especially credit card bills. We know how badly they pinch the pockets if repayment is delayed. There are other general outflows too which we can't avoid, like rent, electricity, staples, clothing purchases, school fees, extra-curricular activities, projects, medicines, transportation costs, etc. It is part of the normal cost of living. But the bigger outflows come in the form of the ever-attractive glamour and luxury items. These lifestyle expenses literally scream out for our attention. The biggest blunder many of us make is to grab the discount offers, even before paying our regular bills.

In this stressful life, we naturally seek entertainment, holidays and other luxuries like branded clothes and accessories, perfumes, modern equipment and appliances, home upgradations, smartphones, vehicles and innumerable other attractive products. All of us aspire for these things. There's nothing wrong with that but beware of unplanned luxury expenses. They eat up big chunks of our income and, by the end of the month, we may be left with NIL or even a negative balance in our account. This may topple your planning even if you have multiple sources of income. Things begin to worsen when we make unplanned purchases of luxury items on EMI. So, hold on to your purse strings!

We saw that there are two ways to achieve our dreams – one is through savings and delayed gratification, and the other is the easier, more tempting '*chota* shortcuts': Personal loans, debt, credit cards, etc. While there are many ways to reach our dreams in a positive way, we generally opt for a quicker way out and damage our personal financial interests.

The secret is to plan for our dreams instead of grabbing them instantly. This may not satisfy all our expectations at once, but it keeps our pocket balance positive. The next important step after paying our basic expenses, and before indulging in those unplanned expenses and liabilities, is to save a significant part of our income every month. A small monthly saving adds up to a lot. And with the help of these savings, we can reduce our debts and start investing wisely.

Why save? Why reduce our liabilities and why invest? Why not spend lavishly and live for today?

We must invest wisely to create a strong asset base that can pay off our liabilities and even our expenses in the future. But to invest and create assets, we need some money. And that money should come from savings first, not from spending or borrowing. One should understand the difference between normal costs (used to buy things) and investment costs (used to improve the future).

You may say, "I don't earn enough money to save." This is surely not true. Every person can put aside at least a small amount every month to start with, and slowly but surely the kitty will grow. No doubt, savings don't bring instant happiness. It makes us feel a bit unhappy and deprived in the beginning. I will say this again: It's 'simple' but not easy. What I want to say even louder is that I feel more secure and happier than when I had absolutely no assets. Assets give confidence, decrease stress and assure us that the future is bright. Once I cultivated the discipline to save a little, I automatically developed the saving habit, which strengthened over time. We are and will be what we do repeatedly. Success or wealth creation is not an event; it is a habit. Make a list of all the wealth creators and you will find that they have a habit of disciplined saving. Their wealth was not achieved overnight through lottery schemes. Creating savings is a slightly difficult path. It's like a bitter pill that we must eat for good health. Investors who save regularly during bad and good times will bleed less during the bad times.

Saving is the first step towards a healthy financial life. But just savings is not enough because money lying in the bank account cannot beat inflation in the long run. To beat inflation and ensure growing returns in the long run, we must create appreciating assets using our savings. We must focus on our return on investment also along with high safety parameters.

Savings is the initial resource to increase that asset base. Simple savings is money put away in a safe place – it is money at rest – whereas, investing puts money at work. It's like sowing a seed that will grow into a tree and bear fruit in the future. Let us focus on growing those trees that can bear fruit for a lifetime, year after year. Yes, we can do it!

Do you think accumulating all the cash in the world will make us rich? No! Even if we have all the cash in the world, it will still not suffice. Guess what? Our cash reserves will be reduced as we spend it. Worse still, its purchasing power decreases due to inflation over time. So, it is not a smart idea to stash away cash in some locker. Just hoarding cash, which used to be a trend a few decades ago, creates a depreciating asset over time.

So, what do we do? Spend, splurge and make merry and spend some more with bank credit? Isn't the EMI route easy and saving every month boring? Buying things through easy EMI schemes gives us instant gratification, but it slowly topples the dream boat. It makes small, tiny holes in our pockets. To return those borrowed funds, we must pay back not just the principal amount but also the interest over many years. Credit card debt corrodes and reduces whatever asset base we have created with great difficulty and patience.

Credit/debt makes everything costlier. Debt increases the overall price of the product we wish to own. For example, a TV which costs Rs 1 lakh can make you shell out at least 150% more through the EMI route. Paying through EMI (equated monthly instalments) means you just converted your transaction from a simple purchase into a loan. There are many other costs like transaction fees, pre-closure fees, etc., and none of them is helpful for the consumer. In our hurry to own a new product, we forget to make these calculations. All these hidden costs drain our funds in the long run, and we end up paying huge amounts for nothing.

If we spend one or two hours every month looking at our flow of funds, it can be a real eye-opener for us. It helped me make a conscious effort to reduce credit purchases and plan my savings and spending. Basically, our focus must change from spending to savings, however small it may be. Subsequently, consider putting those savings into investments that have potential to grow. When we hold on to and protect our investments over a long timeframe, the magic of compounding takes place. In this way, you too can take that quantum leap to financial freedom.

For millions of people who were forced to stop working when Covid-19 struck, when salaries had stopped flowing in, it was only their savings and investments that came to their rescue. The Covid-19 crisis shocked and shook the world economies; the markets and everybody's personal finances went for a toss. Many families were wiped out and those who survived may recall this challenging time and the personal trauma they faced! The earnings from investments become crucial during this trying time.

Investment not only rescues us during emergencies, but it also provides us a secure future and facilitates a graceful retirement.

I listed some of the challenges ahead of me as I worked to bring forth a change in my financial health:

1. How do I build multiple sources of income from limited income?
2. How can I convert my negative cash flow to positive cash flow?
3. How to reduce debt and kickstart savings?
4. I must personally study multiple investment opportunities to create a strong asset base instead of blindly following others.
5. Move from active income to passive income.
6. Aim for an early retirement and a stress-free life

My books again gave me some simple solutions, which I followed actively, to change my destiny and help others do the same. Let me take you through these easy practices.

The 50/20/30 Rule: Track Your Expenses and Savings

This is a simple rule that can be used to manage finances without any complicated calculations, allowing you to allocate accurately for expenses and savings.

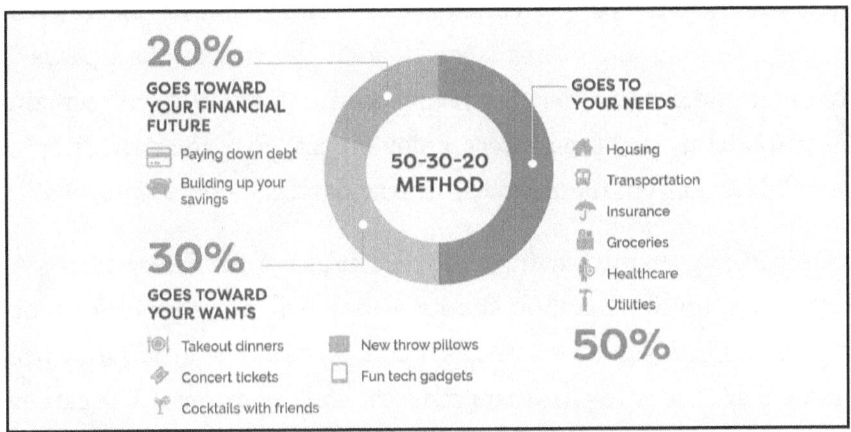

According to the rule, out of every Rs. 100 earned:

- Rs. 50 goes towards expenditures – for basic needs.
- Rs 20 should go into savings without fail – for future goals.
- Rs. 30 can be set aside for indulgences or upgrades – for wants and aspirations.

Yes, why not make it a rule to save 20% first, every month, and then move on to the other things? Pay yourself first. Even the tiny ant knows how to save for a rainy day.

So based on this 50/20/30 principle, we must address most of our regular needs, bills, etc., by using 50% of our earnings. As long as we live in society, we are going to spend 50% on basic needs.

The other 50% we can break it into two separate parts – 20% and 30%. The most sacred part is the 20%. This must and should go into savings immediately. It will help us to initiate an emergency fund for difficult times and create a corpus for long-term asset building and goals. (Initially, you may also wish to start paying off part of your debts with this amount to reduce burdensome loans and borrowings. We will discuss this later.)

So, plan where to put your savings and implement the plan. Do this exercise as if you are paying a bill. No compromise on this one. If we miss this step, we may not even realize how all the money disappears into fulfilling immediate desires. So, savings comes first. With the remaining 30%, you can buy that fancy dress, enjoy a pizza, go to the movies, splurge on a holiday, get gym membership, throw parties, buy gadgets, etc.

Only 20% goes into savings but treat it as sacred. These savings and investments are like bamboo shoots – they will subsequently shoot up and grow *big* into valuable assets. Of course, each age group may need a separate plan. Investing in assets can earn lifelong income. The earlier we start saving, the easier it becomes to create a bigger corpus for the future.

Try to understand that as time moves on, you are going to save more because your income is also going to grow over time. If you still have a few years until retirement, then you can create a big corpus. Today's habit of saving when your income is 1X will help you save more tomorrow when your income becomes 3X. There are innumerable saving options that earn significant returns which we will discuss later.

So, to summarize, the 50/20/30 rule suggests that as soon as we receive our income, we must first save and only then incur expenses. The remaining funds are for entertainment, luxuries and even upgrading our learning. We must keep a sharp watch on how to avoid any unnecessary liabilities. With this rule, we have found an effective and practical method to lay the foundation for creating our asset base. But 'knowledge is hidden power till it is implemented.'

The most important factor is to act on it with consistency. Consistency is the mother of *mastery*, and persistence is how you become legendary. But old habits die hard! From our previous discussion, we saw how most of us rush to satisfy our dreams and, in the process, we create a pile of liabilities that remain with us for life. We learned that loans and credit purchases only increase our expenses substantially. After this detailed discussion, if one itching question still lingers in our minds, like stubborn duct tape, then we must face it.

So let us ask the *'Vikram aur Betaal'* question: "Is it really that bad to use borrowed funds?"

The answer is, "Not at all."

Yes, you may be surprised to hear this. *Is there anything called good debt? How do I escape the trap of debt? How do I always ensure a surplus in my pocket?*

Let us make this clear once and for all.

What Are Good and Bad Debts?

Good debts are those where:

The return on assets acquired using the debt should be better than the cost of the debt. It should not pinch you.

For example, if we take a loan at 7.99% interest to build a house and the house earns a rental income which is more than the interest paid, then it is a good debt. Because the asset earns enough to repay the loan, it bears the burden of repayment on its shoulders.

Bad debts, on the other hand, won't allow you to lift your head or sleep peacefully. The interest repayment eats into your current resources. It completely upsets financial planning. Taking a loan at a higher interest rate to repay another loan, or even playing with leverage like high-risk futures and options hoping to cover old losses are classic examples of bad debt.

Bad debts mostly convert dreams into nightmares, often with disastrous results. A good debt is like the *Kachuva* from the *Kachuva aur Khargosh* story. It makes you the winner eventually.

Let me highlight the **secrets of good debt**:

- Make sure that the return on the asset is better than the interest you pay.
- Avoid paying a heavy interest on depreciating assets.

The backbone of a strong financial plan is to create enough return from our assets, to take care of our liabilities too. You may have to invest some time to digest this. Think about it carefully and work on your liabilities.

The rule of debt: The income earned from the asset which is acquired using a loan should be 2X of the interest paid on servicing the loan. Only then can the debt be termed as a good debt.

If the interest on the loan = X, then the earnings from the asset should be 2X.

There are very few investments whose returns are higher than the cost of the debt. Here is a shopping cart of investments and borrowings in the current scenario. You can take your pick.

Borrowings	Interest Payable	Investment Tools	Earnings Receivable
Home loans	7–8%	FDs, Debt Funds	5.5–6%
Gold loans	9–11%	PPF, SSY	7–7.1%
Personal loans	13–15%	Gold/ Gold ETFs	8–8.5%
Business loans	15–20%	Corporate FDs	10–12%
Credit card loans	33–36%	Realty	Rental income
		Equity and Equity Index Funds	13–15%

We must pick our assets and liabilities carefully on the road to creating wealth. As you can see, there are not many investment tools which can beat the costs of borrowing in the short term or even the long term. The secure and risk-free investment tools grow slowly and so the cost of borrowing is bound to overtake our investments if we are not alert.

Fixed deposit: Not all asset classes appreciate with earnings. Money parked in FDs will earn some interest, but while the capital is safe, your money will not grow. As you can see, by investing only in fixed deposits your investments cannot exceed inflation in the long run. (Inflation rates vary anywhere between 3% and 8% on the higher side. A 4% inflation is said to be the target inflation rate while 6% is a comfortable rate as per the RBI.)

Gold: What about gold? Is it a better option to buy gold? Gold will appreciate, but it won't earn anything if it is in the form of jewellery in the locker. Alternatively, sovereign bonds are a better option compared to gold jewellery. But yes, we cannot wear SGB! The RBI's sovereign bonds earn a small interest rate of 2.5% these days, which is better than no interest at all.

Real estate: Certain kinds of investments have the potential to appreciate and earn income. Real-estate investment is a good example. It can appreciate in the long run and earn rental income regularly. But there are risks involved in each asset class. Real-estate investments need constant monitoring and some degree of maintenance costs as well.

Equity: What about equity? Most people gamble on equities. But if handled with maturity, equity investments can give us a good opportunity to share in the growth and profits of some of the best businesses in the country. Yes, it is possible for stock market investments to give high appreciation but only in the long run. We need to understand that the magic of compounding works only in the long term. In the short term, markets are more volatile and riskier. Good things take time. To get those risk-free compounding returns from the stock market, we must do a bit of study. I will cover this topic in the following chapters.

Most of us are attracted to quick money-making methods, for which the stock market is famous. Lusting after profits, hordes of people plunge into the stock market recklessly and fall easy prey to tipsters and scammers. We experience this negative side of the stock market and lose a lot of money due to insufficient study. Because of this, many people have lost faith in the stock market and label such investments as gambling. However, the stock market is a wonderful opportunity for small investors to invest even small amounts systematically over the long term for huge wealth creation. But many investors miss out on creating wealth because their focus is mostly on the disco lights of short-term profits. They just stalk price movements every minute, instead of learning how to unfold the real potential value of investing in stocks.

Before we learn to invest, let us get back to the topic of quickly returning debts, before they become unmanageable. Every one of us has felt the need to take a debt or loan at some point in life. What we don't realize is that debt management is essential for financial health. As you saw in the chart, debts are costly. So, it's always a good idea to look for ways to reduce debt.

Ways to Reduce Debt:

1. **Windfall strategy:** Whenever I received bonuses or gifts, I would pay off my debts. Yes, bonuses and windfall earnings can be used to repay part of your debt. If there's a chance to reduce a big part of the debt, especially in the first few years of taking the loan, make use of this opportunity, because in the initial years, most of the repayment goes towards paying the interest portion and not the principal amount. Check the

pre-payment clause and get it cleared. It will help to reduce the total burden.

2. **Avalanche strategy:** Another strategy is to quickly pay off those debts with higher interest rates and leave the ones with lower interest to play out slowly. Regardless, the most sensible way is to avoid availing unnecessary credit and focus on increasing your net worth.

3. **Snowball strategy:** This strategy tells you to pay off those debts which are smaller in size to boost your confidence. *Yes, one loan is completed and now I can target another.* One by one, you can wipe out all your loans.

4. **Blizzard strategy:** This strategy is a combination of both strategies discussed earlier – that is, focus on the smallest loan with the highest interest and pay it off. It gives you the benefit of both strategies.

Any strategy that helps you reduce liability is better than no strategy at all.

Focused effort can make it easy to implement this learning in real life. By taking one careful step at a time, you can clear your myths and fears about money management. Undoubtedly, Mr. Patience wins the race. Just look at your current situation and start moving forward with the tools and rules you have studied. **Review – Refresh – Repeat.** Track your financial plan at fixed intervals and organize the actions that you must take to rectify past mistakes.

Let us see if it's possible to afford your dreams while being debt-free. Is it possible to plan for your assets to take care of all your needs and pay for your expenses too in the future?

How do the textbooks define financial freedom?

Financial Freedom

"Financial independence is the status of having enough income to pay one's living expenses for the rest of one's life without having to be employed or dependent on others. Income earned without having to work is commonly referred to as passive income."

'Money working for money' is another name for passive income. Does this seem like a film dialogue? Let's make it real.

The time has come for some real action. The *dishum dishum* in our financial freedom movie begins here with simple yet eye-opening **calculations**. We can do some simple math on how long-term savings grow in different scenarios. Let us bring out the 70 mm picture.

Here are two scenarios.

1ˢᵗ scenario: Let us assume that our Joshila hero is now 30 years old and earning Rs. 1 lakh every month. He decides to start saving for long-term retirement till the age of 60 years. He goes for a stable and safe investment option at 6% interest per annum.

His friend has calculated the result of the investment for him.

Today	Future	Notes
Age: 30 years	Retirement age: 60 years	
Salary: Rs. 100,000	Life of savings: 30 years	
Saving: 20% (Rs. 20,000)	Asset generated: **Rs. 2 Crore**	
Interest: 0.5% (monthly)	Monthly income: **Rs. 100,500**	

So, at 6% annual return, even after 30 years, he will receive only Rs. 500 more than his current salary? This is not at all attractive! Can he survive with this kind of returns? Are there better options? Because 30 years into the future, who knows what the inflation rate, interest rate, medical expenses, etc., will be? If we consider that inflation is going to increase, remember that your income in India will probably grow more than the inflation rate. If you set inflation at 5%, then you should also consider the incremental income, which increases your 20% allocation to the retirement corpus.

So, our hero is not satisfied with this result. He wants to make his money grow because there are several dreams that he wants to achieve over time, like buying a house, going on luxury vacations, etc., from his increasing assets. Thus, he investigates one more scenario.

Scenario 2: This is an option to invest in a well-diversified and well-researched portfolio of the best businesses in the country for long-term wealth creation giving a CAGR return of around 12%.

Today	Future	Notes
Age: 30 years	Retirement age: 60 years	
Salary: Rs.100,000	Life of savings: 30 years	
Savings: 20% (Rs. 20,000)	Asset generated: **Rs. 7 crores**	
Interest: 1% (monthly)	Monthly income: **Rs. 700,000**	

(Disclaimer: These are just estimates but the results can be much better or slightly off based on future events.)

Quite a blockbuster return! Amazing, isn't it? It can come from making the right mix of investment choices. Smart investing! This is called getting smarter or increasing your 'percentage.'

So far, we have got some interesting takeaways from our discussion:

- The first is to make **saving**, however small, a **priority**.
- The second is to **monitor** the quality of **debt** you create.
- The third is to build your skill sets and create **income from multiple sources**.
- The fourth is to **invest** wisely on yourself.
- Finally, we observed that just a small tweak in the growth rate can make such a big difference to the end result. The motto is to **work smart**, not hard.

The next part of our puzzle is to search the pots – **the investment tools.**

The general discussion in our peer groups at the office and among friends is on **the latest investment opportunities** on offer. If someone suggests gold, then everyone is after gold for some time. Soon, the season changes, and crypto mania hits. After some time, people become hysterical about Futures and Options. They over-leverage to the extent of losing everything they own. Again, the fad changes, and everyone starts talking about the next hottest sector, and they all go after sectoral mutual funds. Others float around with hot tips on trending stocks or the joint development of properties. People continue to blindly follow the crowd endlessly.

But apart from the hectic get-rich-quick schemes, are there any safe havens to accelerate growth and earnings without destroying your capital? Most of us don't bother to do any due diligence; we prefer to follow office gossip. These days, SMS, advertisements and digital media too influence us, and we easily fall prey. We don't even understand that many of the influencers are sponsored influencers whose job is to attract us to the sponsoring company. We are misinformed and misled easily because this subject is not in our college syllabus.

Careful selection and a mix of different savings and investment options are the crux of a good financial plan. Mostly, each investor's personal risk appetite will determine which financial asset class is suitable for his financial portfolio. Another way to do this is to match each investment option with your short-term or long-term goals. It's like preparing a *thali* meal, which needs a proper mix of different nutrients. Distributing your savings into several asset classes helps to reduce risk.

The finance books say, "Don't put all your eggs in one basket." God forbid, by chance, if one egg fails, then you won't lose all our hard-earned money. You must plan in such a way that even if one investment fails, the others can take you sufficiently forward.

All of us have a life to live and we reach landmarks like paying for our education, getting married, starting a family, going on holidays, planning for retirement, etc. Along with these usual life goals, wouldn't it be fun to make a dream bucket list too. Ask yourself the following questions: *What do I want in life and by when do I want to get it? In five years, where should I be health-wise, money-wise? At what stage will I need to dip into that education fund? How many years of savings are needed to create that marriage fund?* There are so many questions. Planning is crucial. When you convert your dream into a time-bound plan, it becomes a goal.

A Goal Is an Achievable Destination

Once your list of **goals and investment options** is ready, review your choice of investments based on parameters like growth, earnings, appreciation, risk, consistency, time required, etc. Finally, ensure that the investments you select match your time-bound goals.

We all have our own preferences and comfort zones, but after reading this, you might understand why you should avoid going only after gold, or FDs, or cryptos, etc. If you focus only on one favourite asset class, you miss out on the benefits of the safety that diversification offers.

The solution is to keep one asset class as a base or **benchmark**. By keeping a benchmark, we can check if our personal investments are capable of outperforming or underperforming this benchmark. Let me explain. If, for instance, we take bank fixed deposit as a representative benchmark for all our investments, and if a FD gives, say, 6% interest, then we must try to get at least a 10% return on our investments so that we can do better than the standard and try to beat inflation. Keeping track of it in this fashion, we can give that extra punch to our ROI.

One more observation is that the different varieties of asset classes behave differently in various **economic cycles,** and each has its own advantages and disadvantages. Some are good for long-term goals and some others can be used to meet short-term commitments. The risks and rewards of each segment differ. There are debt funds for long-term needs and liquid funds to park short-term funds. There are PPF and pension funds for retirement and tax savings and term insurance for indemnity and life cover. Study all these asset classes carefully and choose your instruments to match each goal separately. Do not break in and out of your investments and disturb your investment plan too often.

The next exercise is to find a balance between long-term and short-term requirements.

A 50/50 Rule for Investment Is a Good Thumb Rule

It makes sense to divide your entire investment portfolio into two parts: Fifty per cent investment in savings for emergencies and short-term requirements, and 50% investment for long-term goals and retirement.

The whole purpose of savings is for that rainy day when life becomes difficult. But at the same time, our entire savings should not be put on the line just to fund our immediate requirements. This is a crucial part of the plan.

To achieve a sensible balance between short-term emergencies and long-term goal-based investments, we can plan in such a way that 50% of the savings is invested in fixed instruments with low risk and easy liquidity. These investments can be in debt funds, FDs or other fixed securities which are not exposed to volatile market conditions. These funds should be easily withdrawable and used for those goals and emergencies that appear suddenly. Any funds needed in less than a period of 10 years should be in low-risk, fixed securities. This amount will not grow exponentially. Nevertheless, it is safe and gives short-term security and liquidity.

Having planned for short-term needs, we are now free to let the other 50% of funds stay undisturbed in our long-term portfolio. It need not be meddled with to service short-term requirements. This amount should be allowed to reap the returns of long-term compounding, such that we enjoy both the benefits of appreciation and the dividends for generations to come.

This approach keeps our long-term investment plans safe. It gives us enough flexibility to take calculated risks and invest 50% of our money in growing assets like stock markets and real estate and even participate in the long-term growth cycle of our economy. This is how we can prepare and get the best of both worlds, meeting our short and long-term goals.

So, check your investment tools and read the fine print before blindly dumping your hard-earned money into it. Deliberate on the qualities of each asset class and match them to your personal goals. Examine and decide whether the investment should be mapped to your short-term or long-term goals.

Finally, let me share a simple way to monitor your personal financial health at any given point in time: **Net worth calculation**.

For this, make a list of all your assets and liabilities at the current date. It is this calculation which made me take the firm decision to change my habits. I decided to move from being a debt creator to a wealth creator after I recognized that the burden of debt on my shoulder was far heavier, and my asset base was almost NIL even after slogging for many years. I did not have anything valuable to see me through the difficult times. I decided to **reform – perform – transform** my financial picture.

Create your picture and see which side is larger. Do you have more assets or more liabilities?

What Do We Mean by Net Worth?

The sum of all your assets minus the sum of all your liabilities is your net worth.

NETWORTH = (SUM OF ALL ASSETS) – (SUM OF ALL LIABILITIES)

If the answer is a positive number, it means that you always have some surplus funds in your pocket to see you through a difficult period. It means your cash flow is positive! What should be the goal for your net worth? Net worth should not only be positive, but it should be big enough over a period to take care of your required income and goals without working. Income from net worth should generate cash flow consistently for all your needs irrespective of whether you work or not.

Understanding the net worth calculation is a small task, to begin with, but a life-changing one. The chief purpose is to figure out how to keep the funds balance positive under pressing times as well. This means you need to calculate your net worth at least once a year. Registered companies are expected to calculate their balance sheets at the end of every year and declare their quarterly and annual results. So why shouldn't you do it for your personal planning? The net worth sheet is like a personal balance sheet. Just a little focus on these small financial habits can create wonders for you and your family.

So, friends, work on these things:

— Reduce your liabilities and debt.
— Build assets with a better ROA.
— Save consistently every month.
— Try to become smarter in your investments.

Start the smarter, stress-free and tension-free journey towards wealth. Understand your cash flow by recording it. Make a list of your liabilities and work on reducing them. Save consistently and increase your investments. Always ask yourself the following questions: *What is the productivity of my assets? What is the return on the different categories of assets that I hold? Are the returns good?* Become smarter and increase your returns as you go along. Most people pay such a high interest on their liabilities that the return on assets is far from adequate to cover it and their net worth remains negative for a long time. Be alert. Make a list of your assets and liabilities and check it. Keep your returns positive.

A negative net worth gives you 'stress.'

A positive net worth keeps you 'blessed.'

Mr. Warren Buffet said, "Save before you spend."

So far, you have understood Step 1 – managing personal finances, which is the launchpad that sets the foundation for wealth creation from where you can begin your journey on the right track without wasting precious time and money. There are also innumerable books and loads of interesting material on personal finance that you can investigate, but the most important exercise is to kickstart the process. Create that financial plan for yourself as early as possible and start implementing it. Diligently follow your plan.

A firm decision to reduce debt and increase savings is critical. Implement the plan with discipline and patiently start creating an asset base. Select some asset classes to invest in and keep abreast of relevant issues on a regular basis. Slowly, you will learn to adjust your investment portfolio and create the right mix of safe and growing assets.

Do remember the following:

Consistency is the mother of mastery.

You need to start somewhere. Investing a little regularly adds up to a lot.

Just Start Investing.

If you think, *just by investing a small amount today, how can I become rich?* then, you are underestimating your current income. Let me tell you why you shouldn't underestimate your potential. In India the average income grows by 10%, so your income too is bound to grow. Your current salary or business income is going to become 7X in the next 20 years. By investing 20% of your income consistently, your savings proportion also increases. Just remember, the average yearly income of Indians just 10 years ago, in 2013, was Rs. 80,518, while today, in 2023, it is almost Rs. 2 lakhs. In India, we can expect to grow our incomes by 10% even in the coming decades.

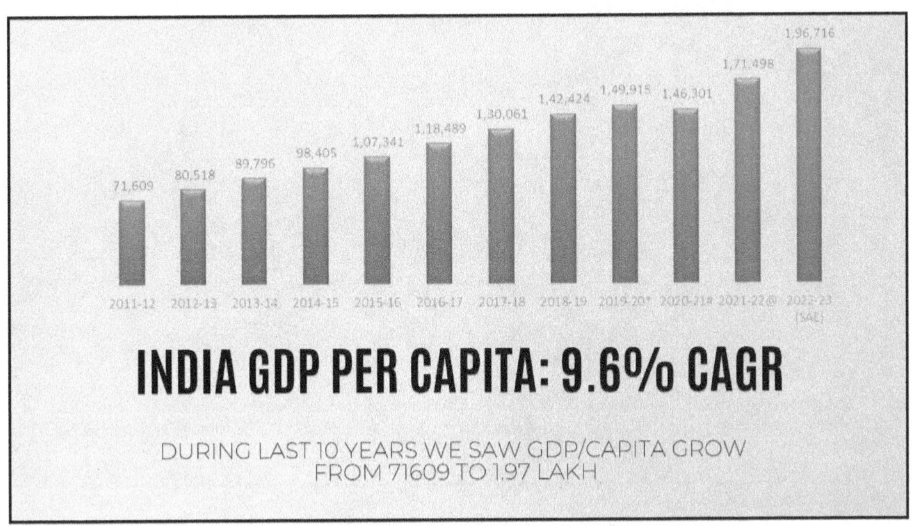

Focus on 'skill-building' to stay ahead and then master it. Any acquired skill works just like 'energy' that your body needs: It helps you during the most testing times. Skill building can help you increase your annual income by more than 10%. Any skill which you acquire can be monetized during a time of need.

Even if you earn just Rs. 20,000 a month, don't underestimate yourself and think that it's too small; you will still see the cash flow of Rs. 2.4 lakh in your account within the first year, Rs. 14.7 lakh in the next five years, Rs. 38.3 lakh in the next 10 years, Rs. 1.4 crore in the next 20 years and around Rs. 4 crore in the next 30 years. Never underestimate yourself. But if this cash flow is not treated properly, it is going to be spent on unnecessary things. Despite good cash flow, we tend to create liabilities instead of assets.

Cash flow is like **water**, divert it for your future, or else it will flow uncontrollably on its own.

If we save just 20% in a plain vanilla investment plan that is a fixed security, our savings over 10 years will be Rs. 11.5 lakh, which is not bad. I did not create any assets during my first 10 years. Why? Because there was no plan. Having no plan is the worst plan. Money came in and money went out. Have a stupid plan, but there should be a plan.

Thus, if a person with a monthly income of just Rs 20,000, saves every month with discipline in a fixed security for 10 years, he will accumulate around Rs. 11.5 lakh in **assets**.

Not bad, right?

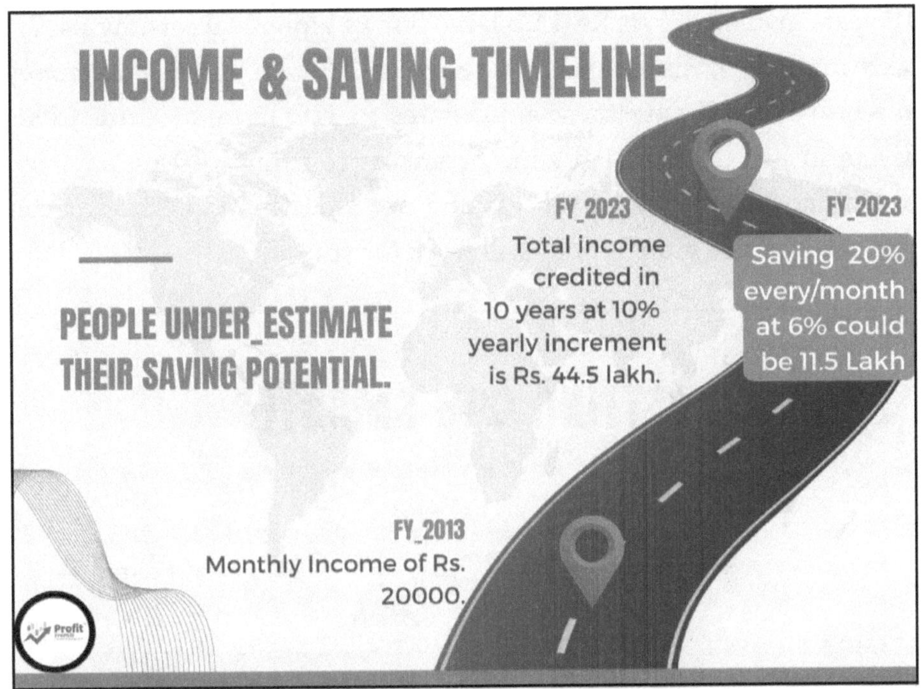

As you've already mastered the art of disciplined investment, now you should start becoming smart in your investments, bit by bit. There's no need to be in a rush. Remember the saying, "Investing a little regularly adds up to a lot."

What do I mean by smart investor? If I get an annual return of 6% but if I'm capable of getting a 9% annual return with the same level of stress, then I've not just become 3% smarter, but in fact, I've become 50% smarter. Mathematics is different from other subjects! This 50% more can make a huge difference to my estimated assets. By continuous learning, we can certainly become 6% or 9% smarter.

Give yourself time to learn, but do not pressure yourself.

Let us assume that over time, this person earning Rs 20,000 gets just 6% smarter than his present-day investments. The difference can be significant. If he continues this exercise of becoming a better investor consistently, then his assets could be around Rs. 15 lakh in

10 years instead of just Rs. 11.5 lakh. For an individual earning Rs. 2.4 lakh annually, if his assets increase by Rs. 3.5 lakh, this is real money at work! Just 6% smartness appreciates to 31% more in terms of his assets in just 10 years! It's important to continue getting smarter. Learning is a continuous process and not a destination. The smarter you become, the more money will work for you.

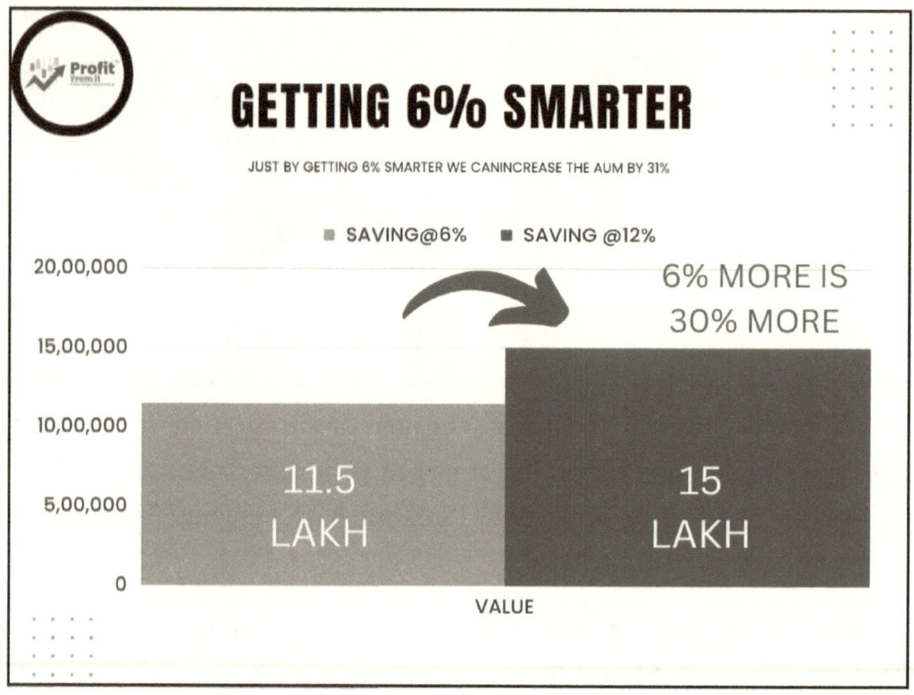

If the same discipline is carried out for the next 20 years, the value of his assets becomes Rs. 52.6 lakh, and after 30 years it will accumulate to Rs. 1.5 crore. Remember, we started the journey at a mere Rs 20,000 a month salary.

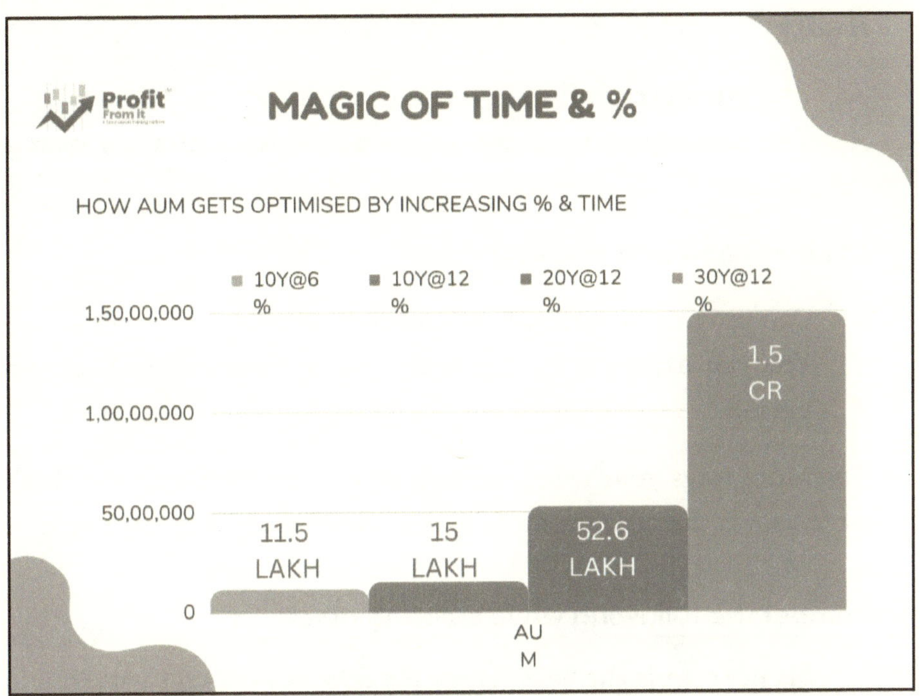

While investing in any asset class, ask yourself some basic questions:

- How much growth can I expect?
- Will this asset provide me consistent cash flow like rent, dividends, interest, or do I just wait for appreciation?

List out the benefits of each investment option. For example:

Gold:

- Appreciates more than inflation over a period.
- Can also be used as jewellery when needed.

Fixed deposits:

- Can either provide cash flow during the term of interest or it can appreciate, not both.

Realty:

- Can provide cash flow in terms of rent.
- You can expect it to appreciate more than inflation over a period.

Business or share market:

- Can provide cash flow in terms of dividends.
- You can expect it to appreciate more than inflation over a period.

The more ways your assets reward you, the better it is, but don't forget to assess the amount of risk associated with the investment.

Remember the following while creating assets:

- Six per cent is the base return for FDs; all other returns should be above this.
- Assets should be well-balanced with risk and reward (50/50 rule).
- Assets should provide lifelong passive income.
- Assets should take care of all costs.

In my experience, random experiments with different asset classes based on other people's recommendations didn't allow me to follow a set plan. I wasted many years running from one asset class to another based on rumours, office gossip, tips and insider information. Intraday trading, stock and index options, cryptos and other speculative get-rich-quick formulas and many other schemes came and went like flavours of the season. These short-term instruments do not help us create long-term wealth. Instead, we become more and more confused and tired, wasting precious time, energy and resources.

After burning my fingers several times and after several wasted years, I got clarity. I realized that long-term investments in the stock markets could give me safe, risk-free and tension-free returns, if

I understood it well and took the right approach. I started to do my own study and began by tracking businesses instead of stock prices. I made time to read the annual reports of companies and listened to the investor conference calls. I collected the data and analyzed the behaviour of each company instead of just stalking its price movements. This gave me wonderful insights on how wealth creator stocks behave when compared to wealth destroyer stocks. Many tricky and confusing patterns which we are unable to discern if we just chase prices can be clearly understood when we analyze businesses according to their demand and industrial sectors.

Equities have a history and potential to deliver better and safer returns over longer periods than other asset classes. Investment in a good company can give both appreciation and consistent income through dividends in the long run. For this to happen, we need to develop a disciplined and informed investment strategy. To get a fairly risk-free and tension-free return, which is adequate to create wealth, we must be prepared to digest the ups and downs of the stock market and have a long-term horizon of at least a 10-year period or more. Once this is clear to us and we focus on the long-term potential of the stock market as a tool to create wealth, we are ready for the next step of our planning: Identifying the fertile soil.

So, if you are ready for the next step, just answer this one important question:

- *Can I create assets that will work for me lifelong?*

If your answer is yes, it means that you are ready to move on to the next step.

This brings us to the next crucial question: Where can we sow the seeds of our investment to reap a robust harvest? Come, let us investigate.

Growing Economy: Invest in a Booming Economy

> Exploration is the engine that drives innovation. Innovation drives economic growth. So, let's all go exploring
>
> **– Edith Widder**

You may ask yourself the following questions: *Why should I look at the country's economy? Is it not enough to focus only on my own personal investment and check whether the land value, gold, fixed deposits or stock prices of my equity portfolios are growing and then just forget it? What has the economy got to do with my portfolio?*

Let me put it another way. What if I say that the proportion of the wealth you are going to create is directly related to the growth rate of the economy. So, would it not be better to examine the economy first before jumping into the markets?

For a moment, let us just imagine the condition of a farmer who must toil day and night on a harsh, dry and barren piece of land, where hardly anything grows well. The poor farmer is forced to work without the support of nature, without good soil, rain or irrigation facilities. Even the best tools or seeds are useless to him. What will his state be after an entire season? What are his chances of enjoying a good harvest? Do you think he will be celebrating with bumper crops, or will he be down in the dumps despite his best efforts?

Would it not have been better if he had checked the fertility of the soil before going through all this trouble? Because, even a few seeds strewn here and there can grow and flourish very well in fertile soil, but the best seeds cannot grow without good soil and monsoons. The same simple logic works for our investments.

Suppose you decide to save month on month hoping to increase your assets every year, but do you think the outcome of your actions depends solely on your efforts? To a large extent, the output of your investments depends on the robustness of your country's economy and even your region's economy. For this very reason, a crucial part of your initial study should be on the growth of the economy rather than how low or high share prices are now. Knowing the country's economic growth, opportunities and challenges ahead will give you clarity on how your investments will grow.

Many people find it a bit tedious, but this study is the primary step. It is a must to look for a growing economy, where you can invest your money and see it grow year on year due to the economic boom. You need to see if the economy is stable and whether it is growing consistently or not. If you invest in a growing economy, the probability of good growth for your investments is high.

So, in this chapter we will try to understand some basic terminology pertaining to the economy and its impact on our investments. You don't need to take any exam in accounting. I myself come from a science background. If becoming familiar with some terminology can improve my investments, then why not do it, right?

First, you must get the relevant data to understand GDP growth. It will give you the necessary confidence to invest in the right place and stay with the investment for long enough till it bears fruit. You must look for fertile soil to plant your seeds. Smart work is needed, not hard work!

Some economies are such that even a little effort brings good results, while some others are debt-ridden and troubled by unfavourable conditions, where even if you struggle for long, your money fails to grow. The growth factor of your country's economy plays an important and strategic role in the way businesses and personal finances flourish. Your country's growth rate will give you a clue as to how fast and how well your personal financial portfolio will grow. Let's see how to check this in a simple way.

The simplest way to measure a country's economic growth rate is through its **GDP**.

What Is GDP?

GDP, or Gross Domestic Product, is a monetary measure of the market value of all the final goods and services produced and sold in a specific time period by a country, generally without double counting the intermediate goods and services used up to produce them. In short, it shows the productivity of a country.

As mentioned, a simple method to see the economic valuation of a country is the GDP.

If we measure an entire country or state by its monetary value, then that value is the gross domestic product or GDP of that nation. It tells us what the productivity of the whole country is in terms of money. It has a direct impact on the lives of citizens, including their prosperity, productivity, opportunities and standard of living.

GDP = Consumption + Investment + Government Spending + Net Exports

If the GDP is low, then it shows insufficient consumer demand, and consequently production is limited, and incomes and job opportunities too are reduced. It is a virtual cycle of degeneration. On the other hand, a good GDP is like an engine for progress.

So, while checking the GDP, it is also important to check the population of the country. Let us understand it better with the help of the two charts given below.

The first one shows some information about the world's population.

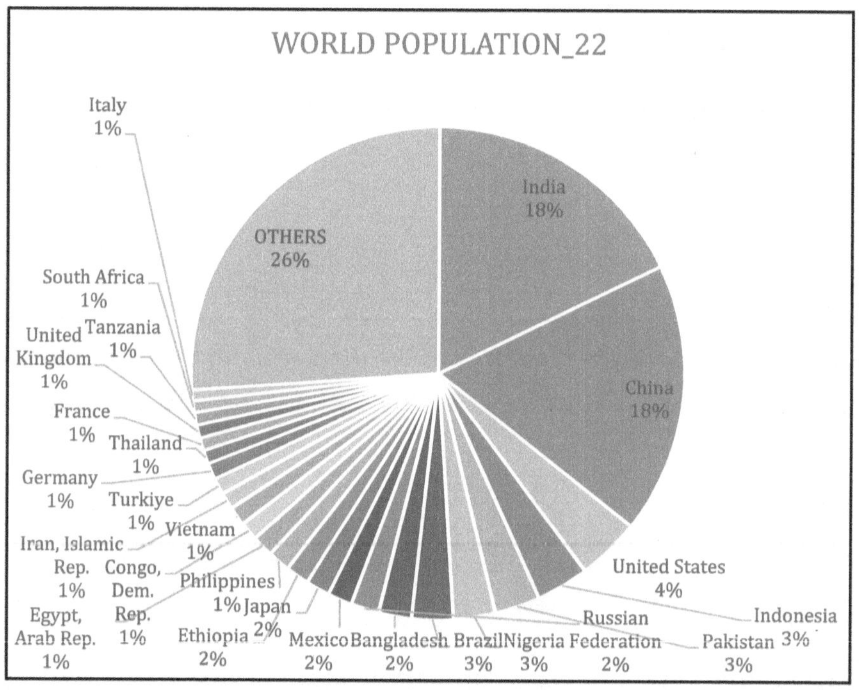

You might be aware that the 800th crore child was born recently. A baby girl born in the Philippines capital Manila has become the 800th crore person in the world, as the global population hit the landmark on Tuesday, November 2022. Yes, today the world population has crossed the 800-crore mark and we can see that India and China alone contribute to 35% of the total world population. Then comes the USA, Indonesia, Pakistan, Brazil, Nigeria and the list goes on.

Now, let's check the productivity of the world and the respective countries in the chart below.

The common belief is that the higher the population of a country, the higher the probability that its productivity is good. But this is not always true, as we can see in the chart below.

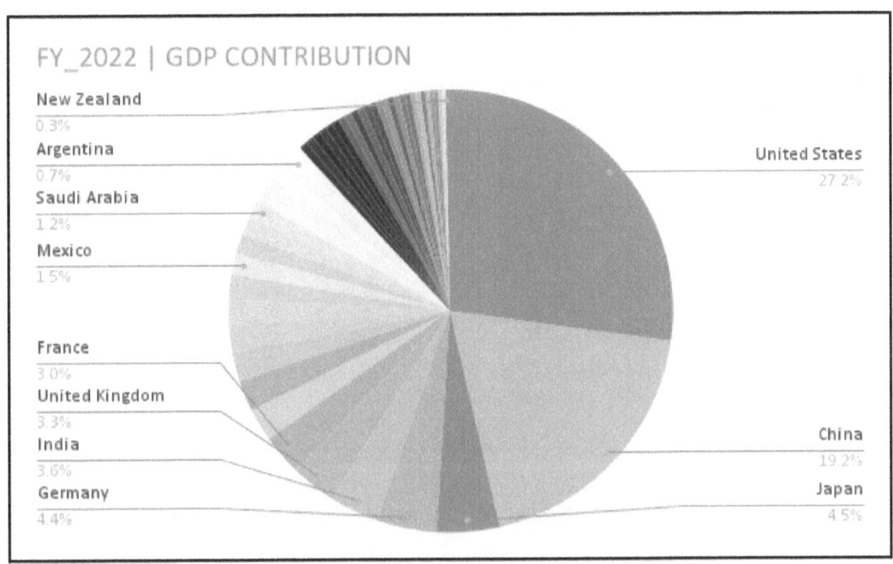

As we can see, the USA is the main GDP contributor, with a 27% share, and China is the second, with around 19% share. Obviously, the correlation is not of population alone. It also matters whether the country's current economic reforms, its financial decisions, social and political atmosphere, etc., provide opportunities for productivity and human potential to grow, year on year.

We can see that the USA accounts for just 4% of the world population, yet it contributes 24% of the world GDP. Why is this so? A few years ago, China, which has a large population just like India, also made a low contribution to world GDP. But today, the story is different. Now China contributes about 19% of the world GDP, even though its population has remained at a similar level. Why is China able to contribute a lot more to the global GDP than India? We must ask ourselves this question before we invest. Let's go back in time to 2,000 years ago and check whether things were the same then. Was India an underperformer and was the US outperforming even then? Let us revisit the past.

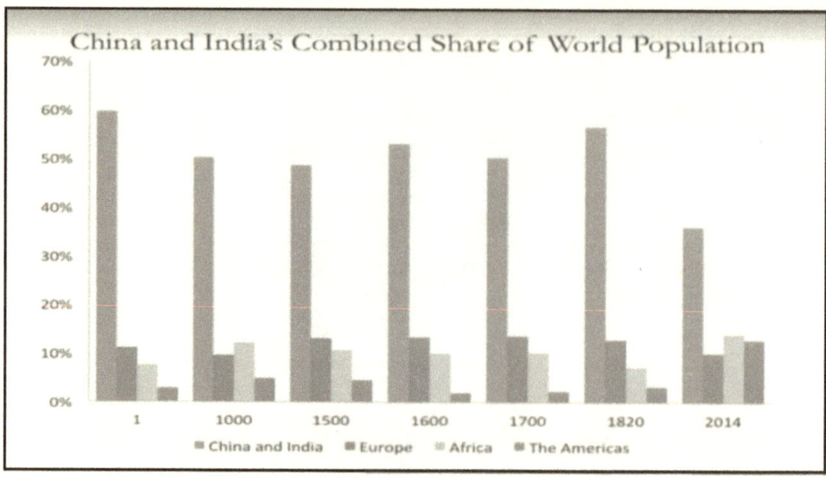

As shown in the chart above, 50% of the world's population was spread across just seven countries. India and China are the most populated countries of the world, and this has been true for many centuries due to the fertile, mineral-rich riverbeds, favourable climatic conditions and natural resources. The above chart shows how not just 200 years ago, but even 2,000 years ago, India and China were the most populated nations of the world. Both countries contributed to around 60% of the total world population even in those days. So, why has this been the case?

It was because India and China were the most fertile places with suitable climatic conditions. Hence, most of the population liked to live in India and China. Historically, countries like India, China, and Rome are the oldest countries with human survival. Some cities in these countries are centuries old and equipped with rich traditions. So, if you think India is a highly populated country because Indians don't control the population, then you're wrong. People liked to live in India, and we used to contribute more to the world productivity than what we are contributing today. This may be hard to believe but it's true. India was loved by the whole world. Now, let us look at the chart below, which looks similar to the chart above but there is a huge difference between the two. Try to spot it.

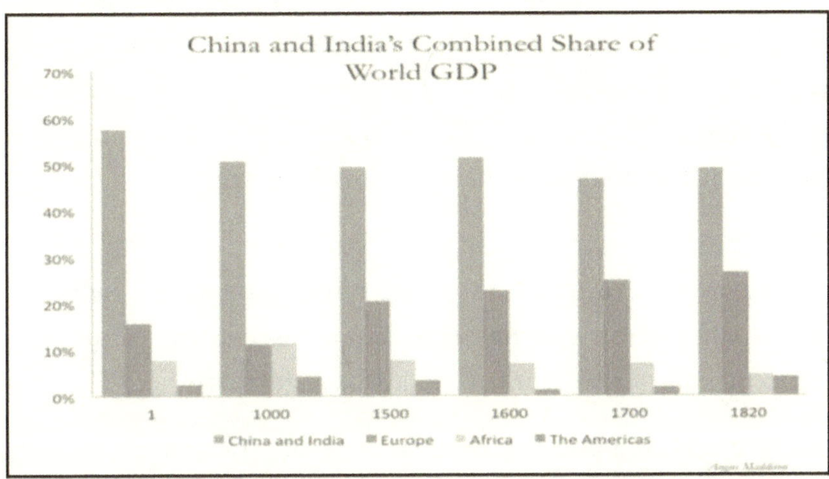

Yes, they look similar, but are not. In fact, the first chart shows the contribution in terms of population and the second shows productivity (GDP). Yes, do not be shocked. India was the most prosperous country in the world! India alone contributed more than 35% of the world GDP and combined with China we contributed around 60%. So yes, we can say that the countries where most people liked to live and used to live were the countries with high GDP. India was rich because of its heritage, education, medicines, tourism and many other factors. This attracted many looters to the country. Yes, India was the 'Golden Bird of the World'.

For thousands of years, even until a few centuries ago, India was known for its gold and metallurgy, spices, fruits and grains, silks, fertile riverbeds, vibrant harvest and peace-loving people. India had already established trade and business links with the rest of the world. When many countries were still in the stone age, India had advanced systems of medicine, education, architecture and philosophy. We even had hundreds of beautiful varieties of weaves in textiles and fabrics, and we were a rich and flourishing economy. Many of the richest cities of the world were situated in India. India was the 'Golden Goose' and conquerors from every part of the world came in the guise of traders to befriend us. They wanted to own our riches, our land, and finally they plundered everything. Looking at things from their perspective, they took a huge risk and came in search of fertile soil. But due to their greed, they destroyed India's economy and for two centuries we were like slaves. After Independence in 1947, and after many ups and downs, the situation is now changing for the better.

If all this is true, then just a few years ago, why were India and China the largest contributors to the number of people living below the poverty line? How did the richest countries become the poorest? It seems to be a fairy tale that turned into a nightmare!

Yes, it's true that you may be rich today, but if you don't stay united you can be broken. Together we were 'Bharat' but when broken, we were divided into regions, languages, castes and much more. The below chart can explain the story better.

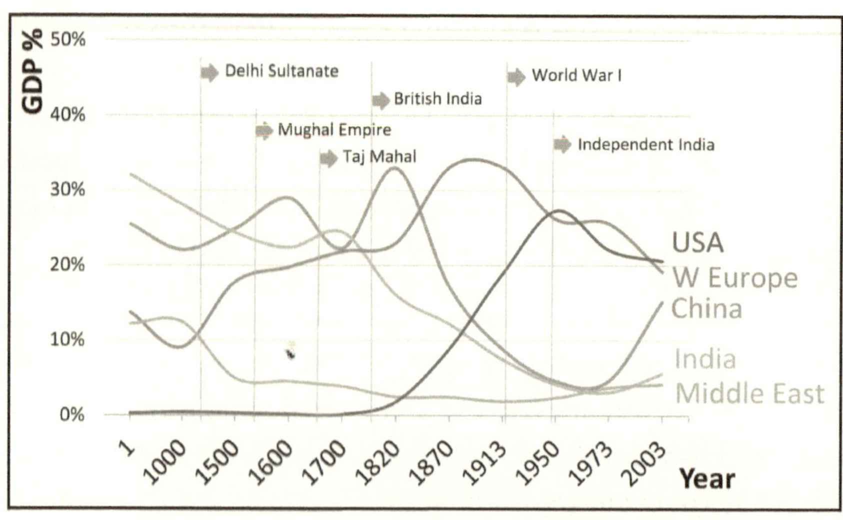

As you can see, India fell from the world's top-most position to the bottom most. There was a time when countries used to see India as the country of innovations and education among other things. How did all this change? There was a time when people around the world wanted to visit India; their world trip would not be complete without a visit to India. But today, Indians want visas to travel to the USA, Australia and Canada. Why? Because people want to live where there is wealth and peace. India was the wealthiest country just 500 years ago. But back then the story was different.

You can see that our wealth attracted so many countries towards us. The most lethal invasion was that of Ghori, which led to the creation of the Delhi Sultanate. The downturn of India started then. We can see the GDP dropping thereafter. After that came the Mughal Empire. By that time, India's contribution to the world GDP was down from 37% to 25%. The Mughal Empire is conventionally said to have been founded in 1526 AD by Babur, a warrior chieftain from what is today known as Uzbekistan. He also mustered up aid from the neighbouring Safavid and Ottoman Empires to defeat the Sultan of Delhi, Ibrahim Lodi, in the First Battle of Panipat. He managed to sweep down the plains of North India as the Mughal imperial structure, which, however, is sometimes dated to 1600, to the rule of Babur's grandson, Akbar. This imperial structure lasted until 1720, shortly after the death of the last major emperor, Aurangzeb, during whose reign the empire also achieved its maximum geographical extent. It was reduced subsequently to the region in and around Old Delhi by 1760.

The empire was formally dissolved by the British Raj after the Indian Rebellion of 1857. With the emergence of British power, the GDP came down from 25% to a mere 3%. Our GDP (productivity) was eaten by the Britishers, and huge wealth from India was transported to Britain. British loot from India was close to $45 trillion in today's monetary value. Over roughly 200 years, the East India Company and the British Raj siphoned at least £9.2 trillion (or $44.6 trillion, since the exchange rate was $4.8 per pound sterling during much of the colonial period). There was virtually no increase in the per capita income between 1900 and 1946, even though India registered the second largest export surplus earnings in the world for three decades before 1929. Yes, it is surprising, but it is the hard truth.

From the world's richest country, India became one of the poorest. After a prolonged fight, India got Independence in 1947, but by that time, everything was looted, and India was left only with horror stories. No money, no education and no health. We were at ground zero level. The only thing we had at that time was hope.

At the time of India's Independence, our share of GDP dropped to a mere 2% from being the world's highest at 37%. Our GDP/capita was among the lowest of all countries and the world's below poverty line population mostly resided in India and China.

India was the leader during the First Agricultural Revolution. During the 18th and 19th centuries, the world saw the Industrial Revolution 1.0, where they learned to produce from primary products like textiles, iron, etc. This was followed by the Second Industrial Revolution which was all about mass production assembly lines. This was when India was fighting for Independence and was left behind during both revolutions. Companies started producing goods and the world even saw the boom of the automobile industry with mass production. India was not in the picture during this revolution. India could not do well in manufacturing compared to the rest of the world. This was the time when countries like Japan, the USA, and Germany started to grow. Just before the dawn of the 19th century, the UK was the world leader, but post World War 1, as the Industrial Revolution started, we saw countries like the USA and Japan starting to accelerate ahead of the UK. The USA moved ahead of the UK during the early 20th century, while Japan overtook the UK around the mid-20th century.

The world order changed due to the Industrial Revolution and the two World Wars. The 20th century definitely belonged to the USA and Japan. The USA overtook the UK as industrialization 1.0 started. The dominance of the UK decreased by 1970 as Germany, Japan and France also proceeded to overtake the UK.

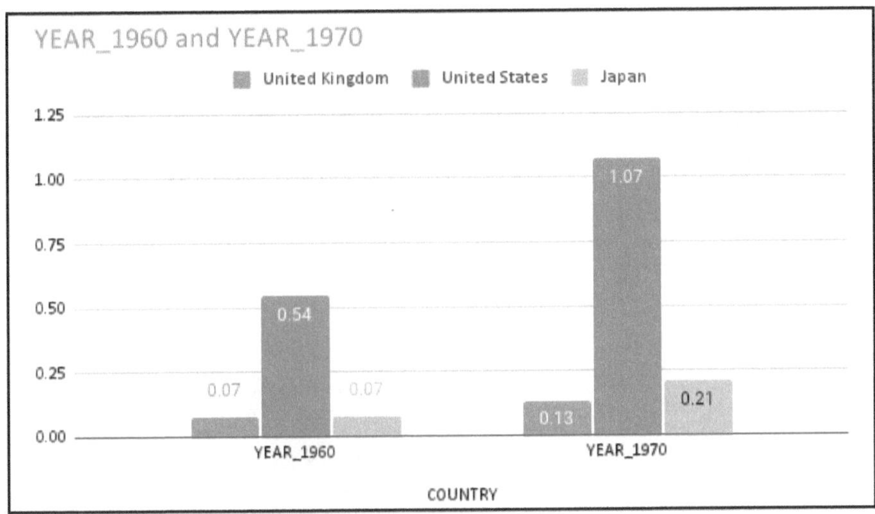

The world leader of the 19th century was not replaced by several others as we can see in the below chart.

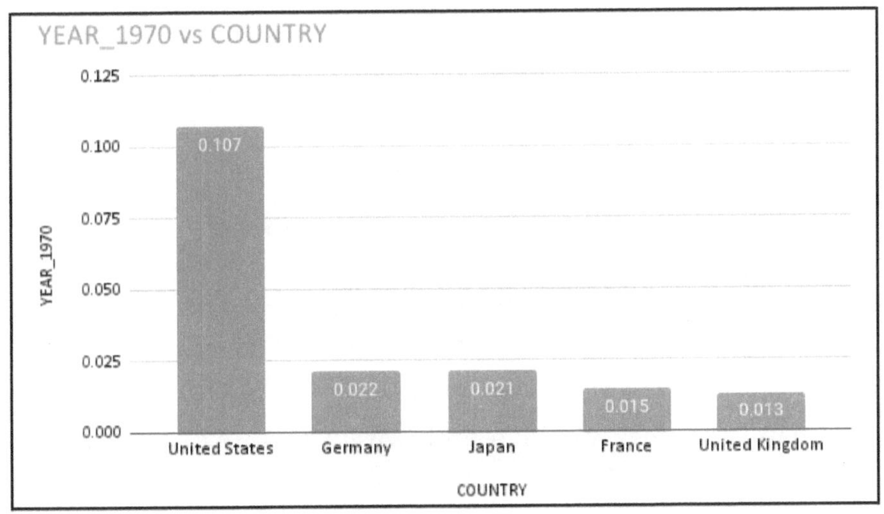

The Industrial Revolution helped Germany, Japan and France move ahead of the UK, but the US was way ahead of the UK. In fact, during the Industrial Revolution, many companies witnessed a manufacturing boom, which was initially led by the textile mills and steel industry. India lagged during that period. In fact, there was a huge divergence, as in countries like Japan, local manufacturing was government-supported and they levied high tax on imports to support the locals. But it was the opposite in India as it was British India. High taxes were levied on local manufactures and imports from Britain were supported. This made Indian businesses struggle and there was no scope for growth. While Japan and many other countries were growing during the Industrial Revolution, India's growth was declining.

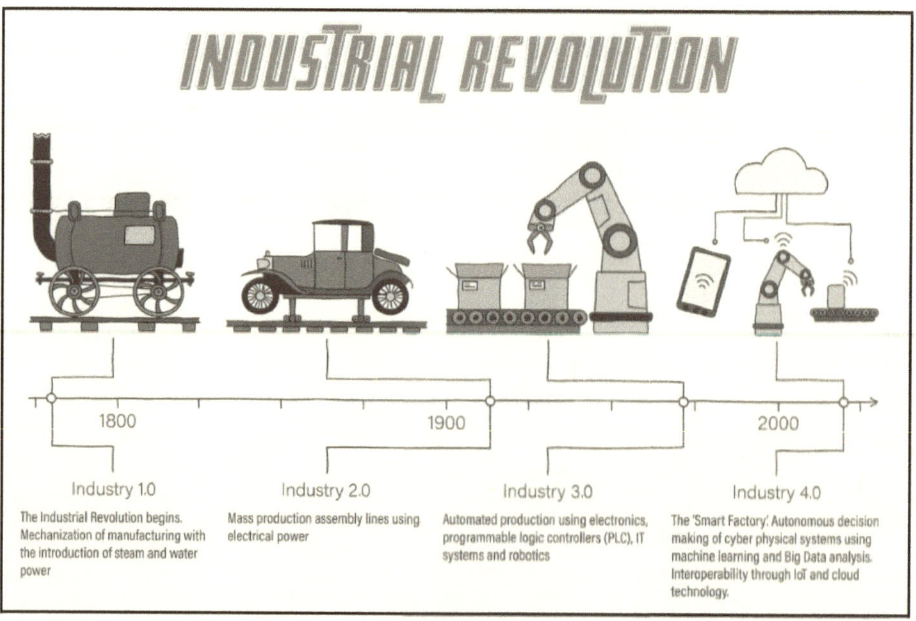

World Wars I and II, which started in 1914 and lasted till 1945, was bad news for the world, but great news for Indian companies, as the demand for steel was high and Britain was unable to supply in

India. This gave Indian manufacturers the opportunity to cater to the local demand. We saw Tata Steel, the local Indian steel manufacturing company, benefiting from this demand. But due to harsh British policies against India, which aimed to supress the locals and encourage imports from Britain, India had remained backward for years, when the rest of the world was developing.

1980_GDP_TR_USD

☒ 1980_GDP_TR_USD

Rank	Country	1980_GDP_TR_USD
1	United States	2.9
2	Japan	1.1
3	Germany	1
4	France	0.7
5	United...	0.6
6	Italy	0.5
7	Canada	0.3
8	Brazil	0.2
9	Spain	0.2
10	Mexico	0.2
11	Netherlands	0.2
12	China	0.2
13	India	0.2
14	Saudi Arabia	0.2
15	Australia	0.1
16	Sweden	0.1
17	Belgium	0.1
18	Switzerland	0.1
19	Argentina	0.1
20	Indonesia	0.1

Poverty contribution and world growth era?

Till 1980, if we look at the top 20 countries' ranking, the US leads the world with 26% contribution to the world GDP. Japan stands second due to their favourable manufacturing policies. Japan, Germany and France were the leading countries, while the UK ranked 5th. India and China, which were the leading contributors to the GDP till the 18th century, were not even in the top 10. India's and China's GDPs were similar. This was a time when both countries together contributed to 65% of the world's poverty. This was due to the high population and low GDP, resulting in low GDP/capita. China had a population of around 98 crores in 1980, while India's was 70 crores. Thus, China contributed to 43% of the world's extremely poor population, while India's contribution stood at 22%. Keep in mind that the two countries that once contributed 65% of the world GDP now contributed only 3.3% of the global GDP, although they accounted for 40% of the world's population. Over the years, the population increased but productivity remained low, pushing the large population further into extreme poverty. So, in 1980, 65% of the extremely poor population lived in India and China. How quickly we can go from being the best to the worst if we don't take care of our resources!

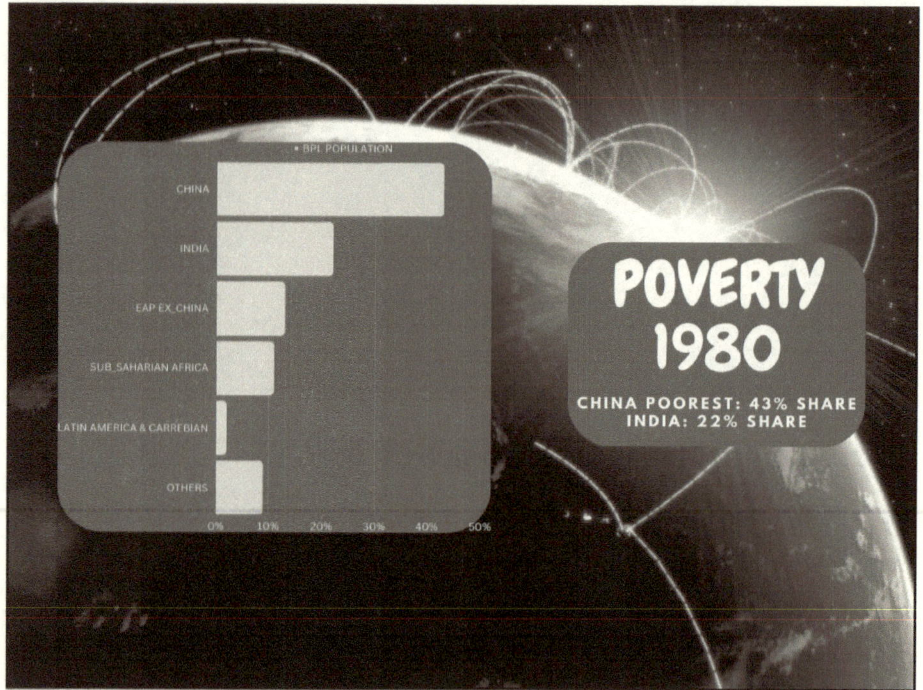

Till 1980, China and India were the top poverty contributors, but this didn't continue for long. China introduced local manufacturing policies and several reforms which lead to the Chinese boom. Reforms helped Chinese GDP grow and its positive spill over effect was seen in per capita earnings of the Chinese. The increasing GDP helped China rescue the extremely poor people from poverty. The chart for 2005 below clearly explains this transformation.

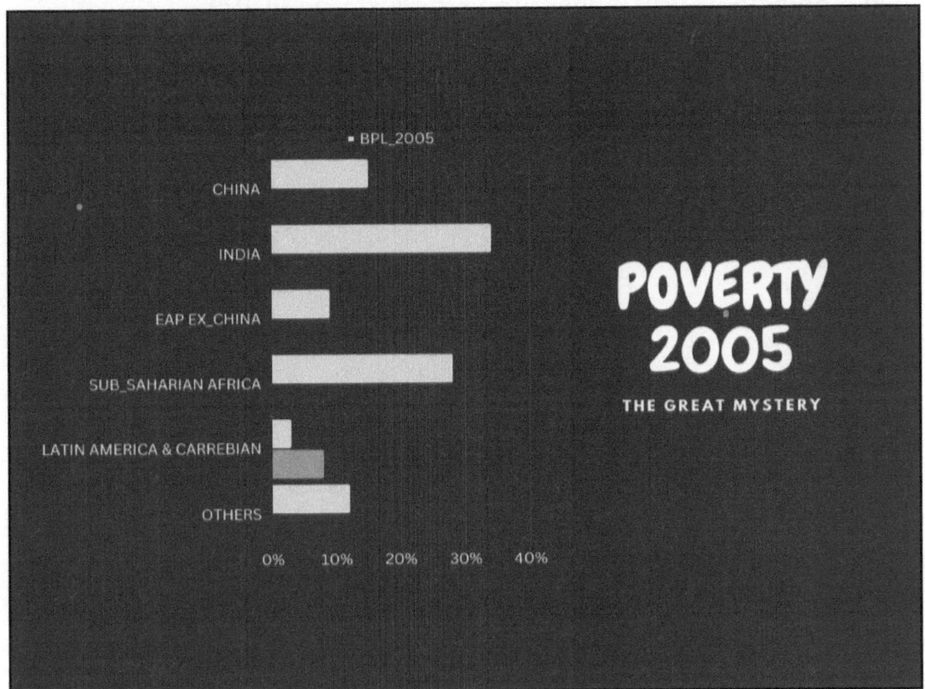

During the beginning of the 21st century, China returned to growth and reduced its contribution to world poverty, while the No. 1 poverty tag, shifted from China to India. Thus, at the beginning of the 21st century, India was the top poverty contributor. Why did this happen? Why was China able to benefit from their human resources while India lagged?

Let us see what happened in India. Undoubtedly, the age of kings and queens, merchants and marauders was over, but the transition period from Independence to the 20th century turned out to be very difficult. We were burdened with a large part of the population struggling below the poverty line. There was malnourishment, poor health, and lack of education. Power politics, corruption, chaos and licence Raj had become the norm. Post-Independence, problems of over-regulation, an unresponsive and inefficient bureaucracy, and the discouragement of foreign investment impeded development. All this made India poorer till bigger problems surfaced in 1991.

The below chart shows us how the world was growing but India was underperforming and eventually missed the big growth phase.

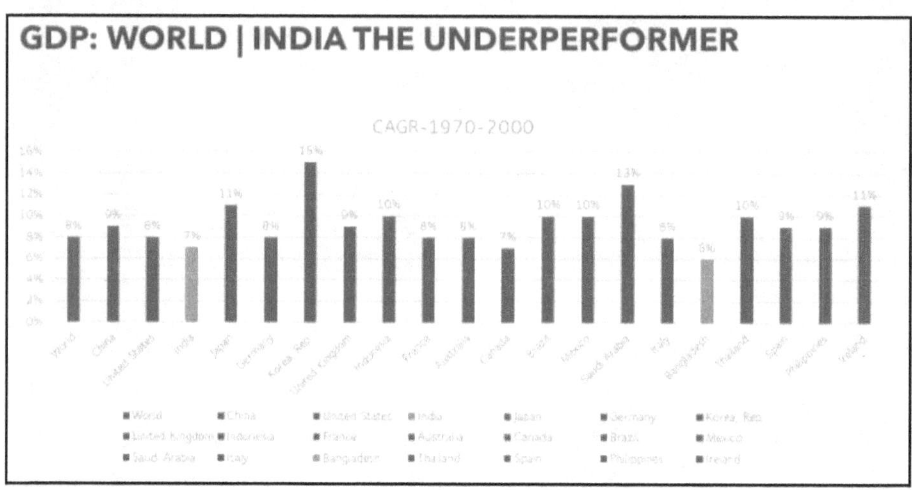

In 1991, India's trade deficit made us pledge our gold reserves. By June 1991, India had less than $1 billion Forex reserves, just sufficient to meet import requirements for a period of three weeks. It did not have enough Forex reserves to conduct business with the world. The country was on the verge of defaulting on its International Debt Obligations. Investors pulled out their money. As per the IMF, the 1991 crisis in India is believed to have been caused mainly by high fiscal deficits, the loss of confidence in the government and mounting current account deficits. We sought a loan from the IMF and learned our lessons never to repeat these financial mistakes again.

After the new economic policy of 1991, India focused on building foreign exchange reserves, removing market restrictions, and increasing the exchange of goods, services, capital, human resources and technology worldwide, thus encouraging the economy's growth. The direct impact of these reforms, like privatization of industrial sectors, liberalization and globalization of the economy, are now bearing fruit, and it has put India on the trajectory to becoming a phenomenal growth story. The below flowchart explains the economic reforms.

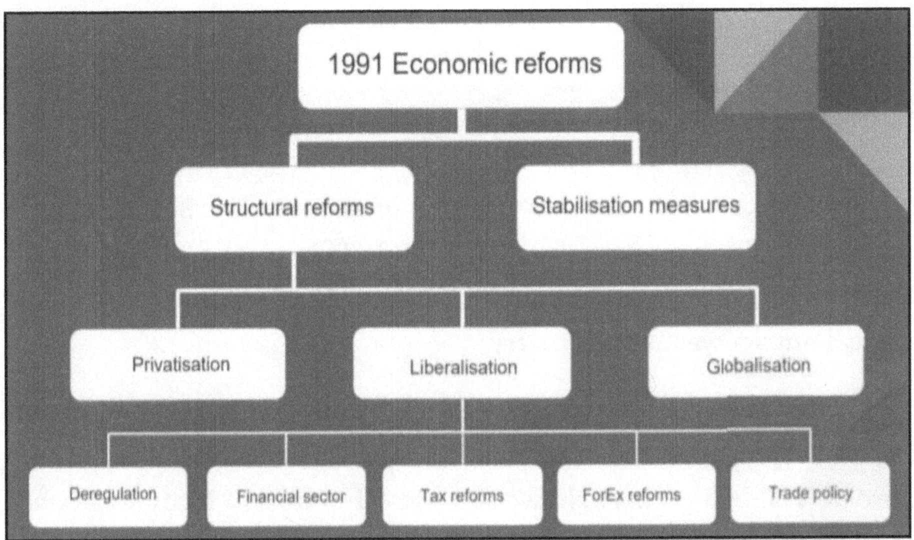

This was the important turning point for India. It ended the licence Raj and gave birth to today's modern industrialization, which has boosted employment. Previously, people were dependent on government employment. Today, large and powerful corporations, efficient markets, technological prowess, strong political leadership and informed public opinion run our economy. The entire canvas has changed.

Whatever happened post 1991 is very important. The reforms introduced gave a boost to the economy. Today, there are many private enterprises which provide better employment avenues than the government. The economy is not dependent on the government. This has created better employment opportunities and its spill over is seen in the increasing GDP/capita.

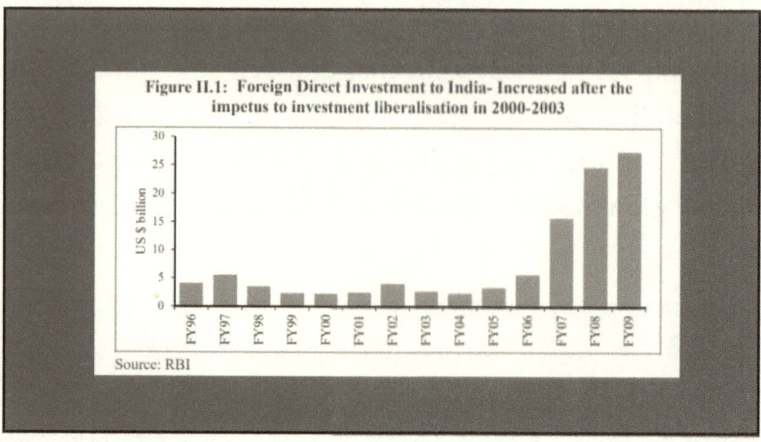

Figure II.1: Foreign Direct Investment to India- Increased after the impetus to investment liberalisation in 2000-2003

Foreign direct investment in India increased after the impetus to investment liberalization in 2002–2003. This further strengthened the economy. The decade of 1991–2001 was the decade of reforms and its real impact was felt a bit later.

At one point in time, due to a lack of opportunities and income imbalance, most of the smart brains looked for better opportunities abroad. The below chart showcases the difference in income between the US and India seen around 1991. It's true that the difference in income was around 80X. Post reforms, the gap has reduced. Right now, the difference is 30X, which is the lowest it's ever been in six decades. Day by day, the gap is reducing.

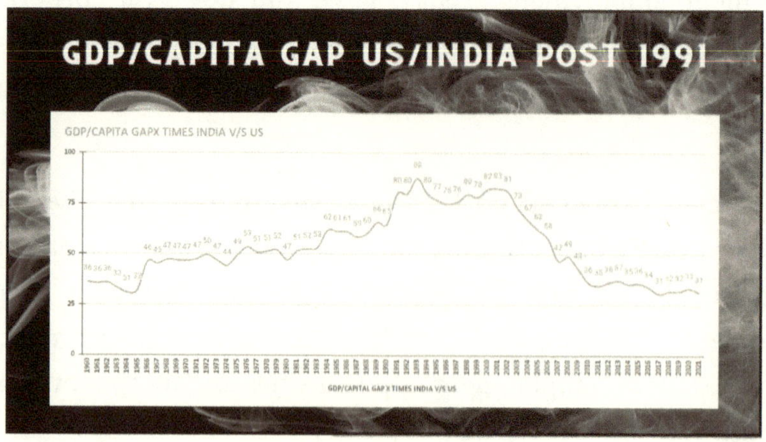

The growing GDP has helped India outperform other countries post the reforms. India, which stood 17th in 1991, made it to the world's top 10 economies in 2010. Today, as we talk, we have jumped to the 5th place, overtaking the UK. India proudly overtook the UK again after 200 years. What a proud moment for India! The country is now expected to jump to the 3rd position by 2030, overtaking Germany and Japan. Get ready, it's India's time now.

When India was just recovering from the 1991 shock and reforms were being put in place, we saw some more shocks between 1998 and 2002.

More Shocks Post 1991

Nuclear device testing by India in 1998 was followed by sanctions. While the banking and corporate sector deleveraged and repaired their balance sheets, we faced two successive droughts. Simultaneously, in the US, we saw a technology bust and the 9/11 tragedy, which affected the whole world.

This led to a big drop in world markets, with a 50% drop in S&P 500 during the same time.

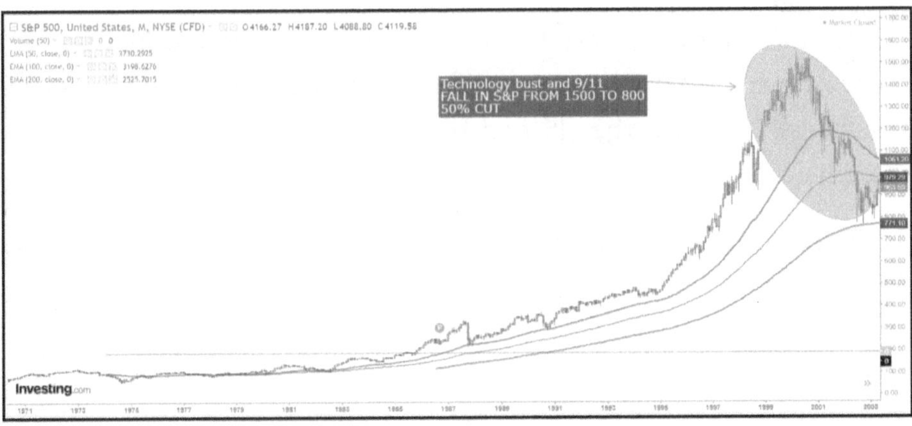

Indian markets also reacted similarly as we can see a 50% drop in Nifty during that time. Before we could reap the fruits of reforms, our markets were once again trapped.

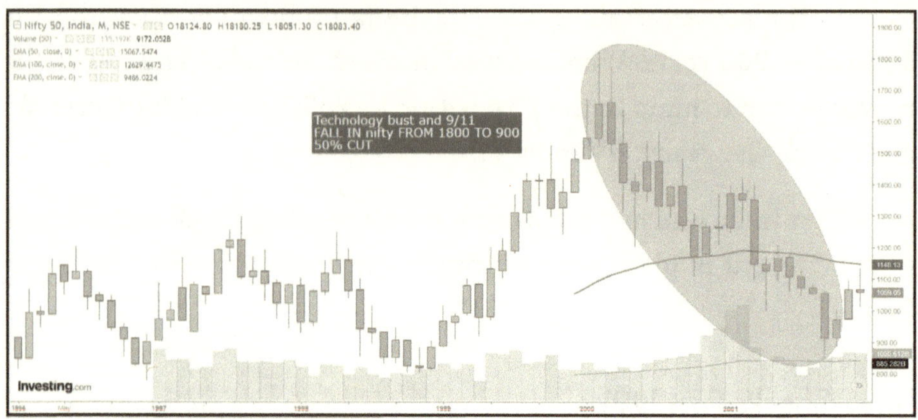

Reforms in Place

Despite these ups and downs in the world markets, India kept busy with reforms between 1998 and 2002. De-regulation of interest rates, privatization, asset recovery of banks, infrastructure (Golden Quadrilateral), the FRBM Act, etc., were some of the reforms put in place during this ongoing shock to the economy which helped India later.

In both markets, post the big fall, reforms were ongoing, and these reforms started paying off later. Consequently, we witnessed a huge rally in both the US and Indian markets, as depicted in the chart below.

Rally from 800 to 1,600 was seen in S&P500.

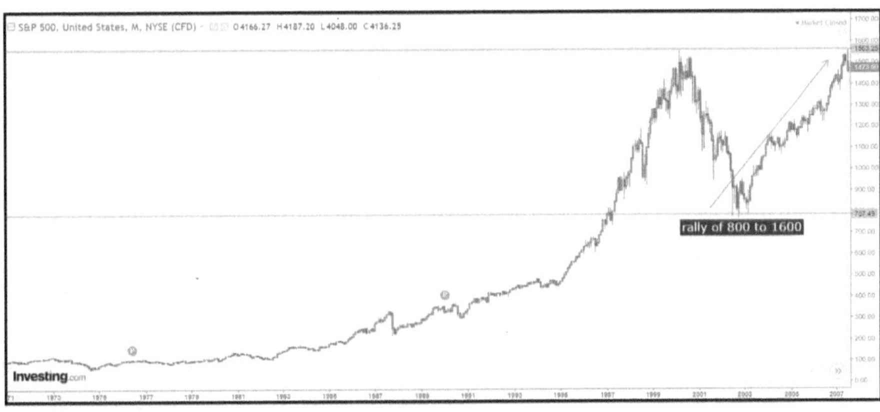

Similarly in the India market, Nifty saw a rally from 100 to 6,000, post reforms during FY2003 to FY2007.

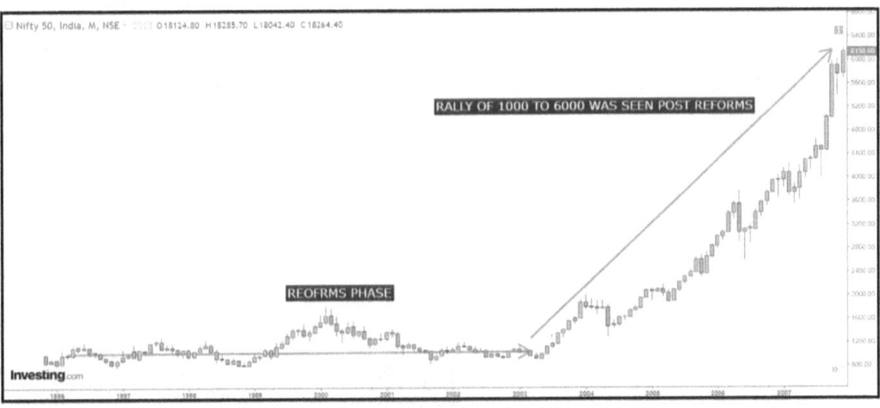

This clearly suggests that the effects of the reforms introduced to boost the economy became directly visible in the stock market index. It may have taken some time to reflect, but it did eventually show up.

A Similar Phase of Reforms is Going On

Currently, India is witnessing a similar phase of reforms. Many structural reforms were initiated between 2014 and 2020. Some noteworthy changes include the unique identity card (AADHAR), financial inclusion, GST leading to the formal market, IBC code for banking, more privatization, tax rates rationalization and tax admin reforms, decriminalization of offences, vaccine rollout, expenditure management reforms, AtmaNirbhar Bharat, Public Digital Infra and many others.

Simultaneously, we experienced some large-scale shocks too. Covid-19, war, inflation, etc., had a spill over effect on interest rates. One-off shocks also delayed growth, but later, growth became visible between 2003 and 2007. This time around also we may see strong growth in India as the shocks reduce. India is all set to jump to new heights again, thanks to the numerous reforms.

We can see that we underperformed when compared to many other countries during the 20th century, but in the 21st century, India is clearly ahead.

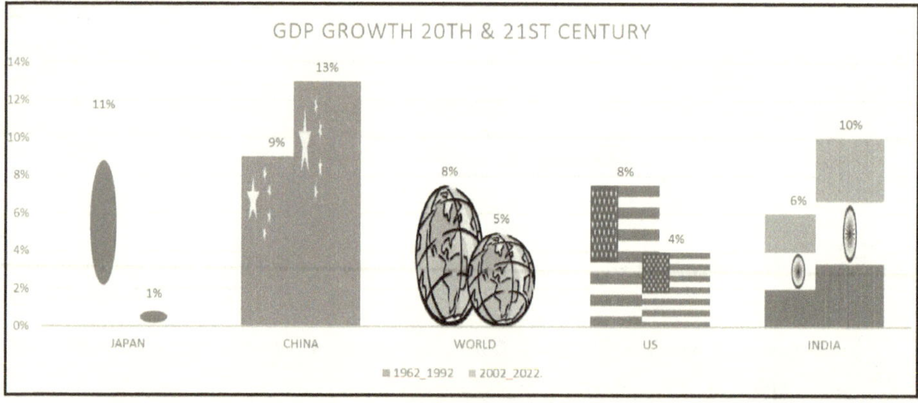

The 21st century seems to be India's century. India is outperforming major economies.

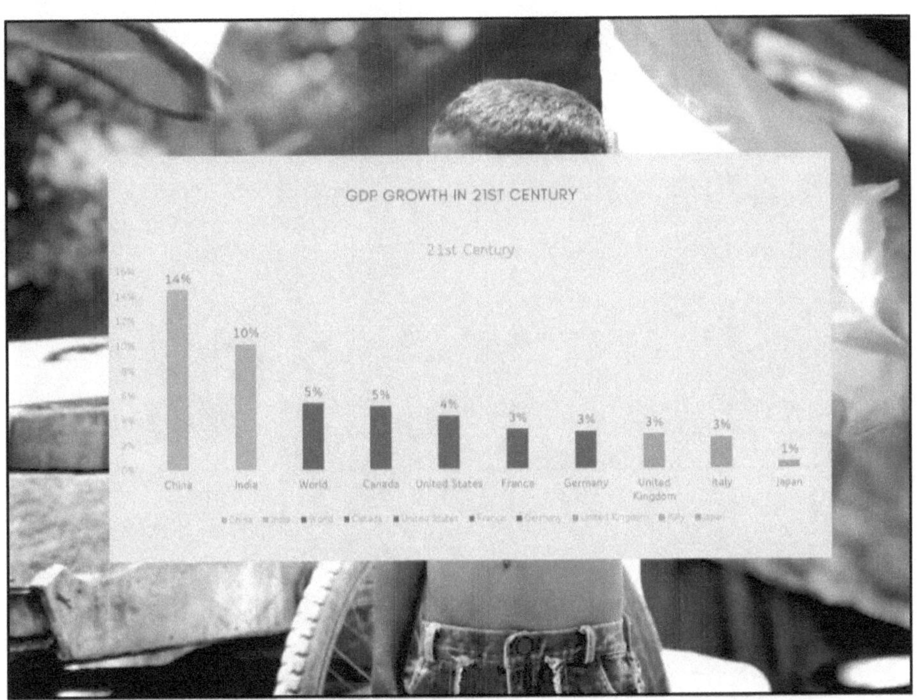

During the 20th century, the US was the largest contributor of growth to the world economy. In 1960, the world GDP was 1.4 trillion USD. By 2000, it grew by 20X and became 30 trillion USD. The US, which was at 0.5 trillion USD, grew by 20X to reach 10.3 trillion by 2000. Yes, countries like the US and Japan were large contributors of growth to the world.

The 21st century tells a different story. In 2001, the world GDP was at 34 trillion USD. Now it is 97 trillion USD – a 3X expansion over the last 20 years. India's GDP in 2001 was 0.5 trillion USD, which is now 3.2 trillion USD, a growth of 7X. Thus, in the 21st century, India is one of the major contributors to world growth.

The below chart clearly tells us this story.

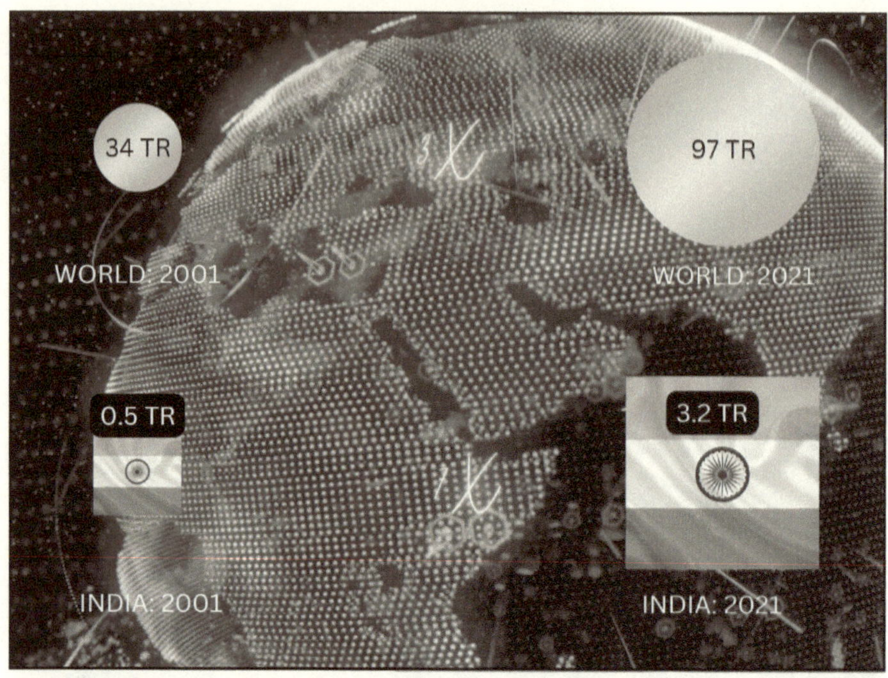

34 TR
97 TR
WORLD: 2001
WORLD: 2021
0.5 TR
3.2 TR
INDIA: 2001
INDIA: 2021

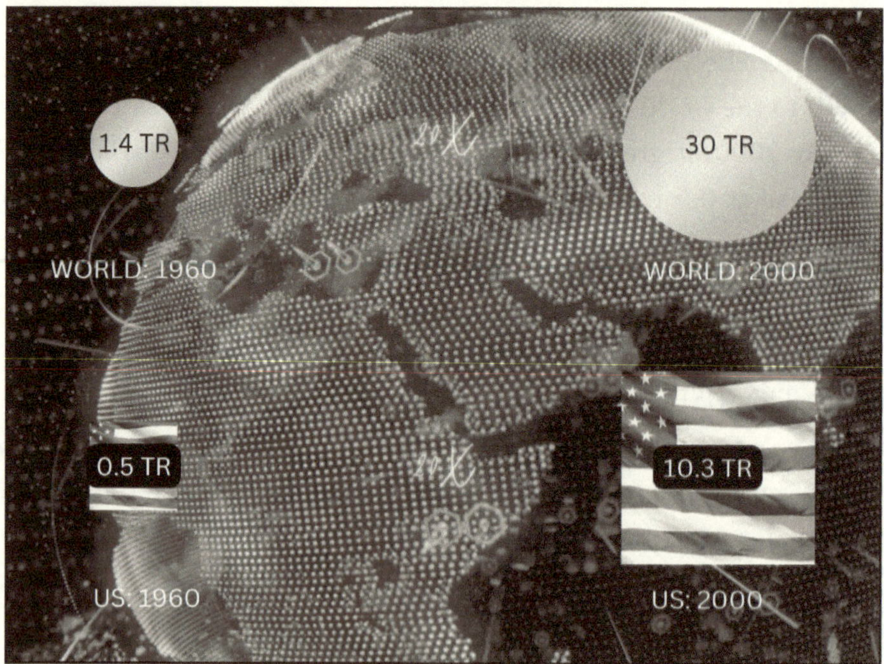

1.4 TR
30 TR
WORLD: 1960
WORLD: 2000
0.5 TR
10.3 TR
US: 1960
US: 2000

The growth of the US, Europe, and Japan during the 20th century helped companies situated in these countries to grow bigger. Subsequently, companies from China entered this elite club during the 21st century, as they were the fastest growing major economy post 1980. In 2010, Chinese companies like PetroChina, ICBC and China Construction Bank made it to the world's s largest companies list. A country that nurtures growth helps its companies grow large. This is reflected in American, European, and Japanese companies, and most recently, Chinese companies too. The below figure lists the largest companies in 2010.

Rank	COMPANY	COUNTRY
1	ExxonMobil	United States
2	PetroChina	China
3	Apple	United States
4	BHP Billiton	United Kingdom
5	Microsoft	United States
6	ICBC	China
7	Petrobras	Brazil
8	China Construction Bank	China
9	Royal Dutch Shell	United Kingdom
10	NESTLE	Switzerland

2010
TOP 10 COMPANIES

ENTRY OF DRAGON

Now what? What does the future hold?

India is estimated to grow more than all the other major economies in the world as per the IMF.

Listed below are the latest estimates by the IMF during the challenging time of war, inflation and interest rate hikes. As per the IMF, world growth will witness challenging times for the next five years. In fact, we are going to see one of the slowest five-year growths in the world. But at the same time, India is expected to outperform the world. We are going to outperform advanced economies and even major developing economies! Just have a look at their projections.

Latest World Economic Outlook Growth Projections

		PROJECTIONS	
(Real GDP, annual percent change)	2022	2023	2024
World Output	3.4	2.8	3.0
Advanced Economies	2.7	1.3	1.4
United States	2.1	1.6	1.1
Euro Area	3.5	0.8	1.4
Germany	1.8	-0.1	1.1
France	2.6	0.7	1.3
Italy	3.7	0.7	0.8
Spain	5.5	1.5	2.0
Japan	1.1	1.3	1.0
United Kingdom	4.0	-0.3	1.0
Canada	3.4	1.5	1.5
Other Advanced Economies	2.6	1.8	2.2
Emerging Market and Developing Economies	4.0	3.9	4.2
Emerging and Developing Asia	4.4	5.3	5.1
China	3.0	5.2	4.5
India	6.8	5.9	6.3
Emerging and Developing Europe	0.8	1.2	2.5
Russia	-2.1	0.7	1.3
Latin America and the Caribbean	4.0	1.6	2.2
Brazil	2.9	0.9	1.5
Mexico	3.1	1.8	1.6
Middle East and Central Asia	5.3	2.9	3.5
Saudi Arabia	8.7	3.1	3.1
Sub-Saharan Africa	3.9	3.6	4.2
Nigeria	3.3	3.2	3.0
South Africa	2.0	0.1	1.8
Memorandum			
Emerging Market and Middle-Income Economies	3.9	3.9	4.0
Low-Income Developing Countries	5.0	4.7	5.4

2023 has been a challenging year for the world where:

- Ninety per cent of the advanced economies projected a decline in their growth.
- Close to USD 300 billion fresh funding was provided to 96 countries due to the challenges the world faced.
- Fifteen per cent of the low-income countries are already in debt distress.
- Forty-five per cent of the low-income countries are facing high debt vulnerabilities.
- Twenty-five per cent of the emerging economies are at high risk. We saw examples of Pakistan, Sri Lanka and Bangladesh recently.

During these challenging times, the IMF estimates that half of the global growth is expected to come from China and India. Yes, the world has high hopes for our country, and this is India's time. India is going to be in a bright spot for the next few decades. Notice India's special place in the chart published by the IMF.

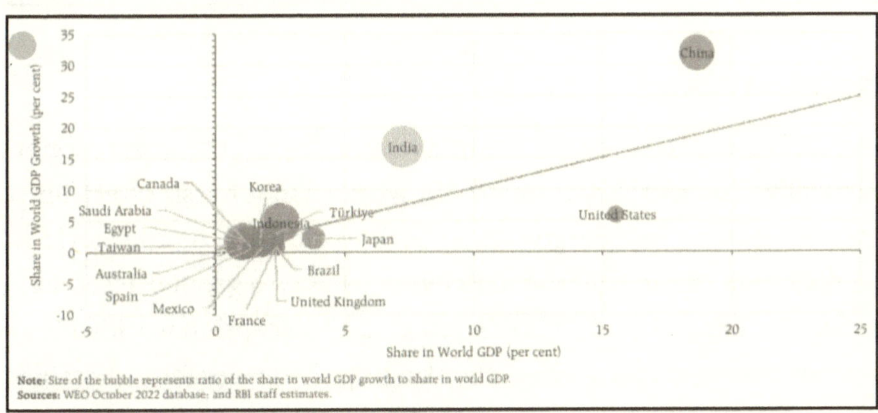

Note: Size of the bubble represents ratio of the share in world GDP growth to share in world GDP.
Sources: WEO October 2022 database; and RBI staff estimates.

Yes, we missed the 19th and 20th centuries, and we were 30 years behind countries which grew fast. But the 21st century is India's century, and we are not going to miss out this time.

Over the last 10 years, India's GDP growth rate stood at 9.3%, which has helped our GDP/capita enter double digits at 11%. We can see this growth trajectory in the chart below.

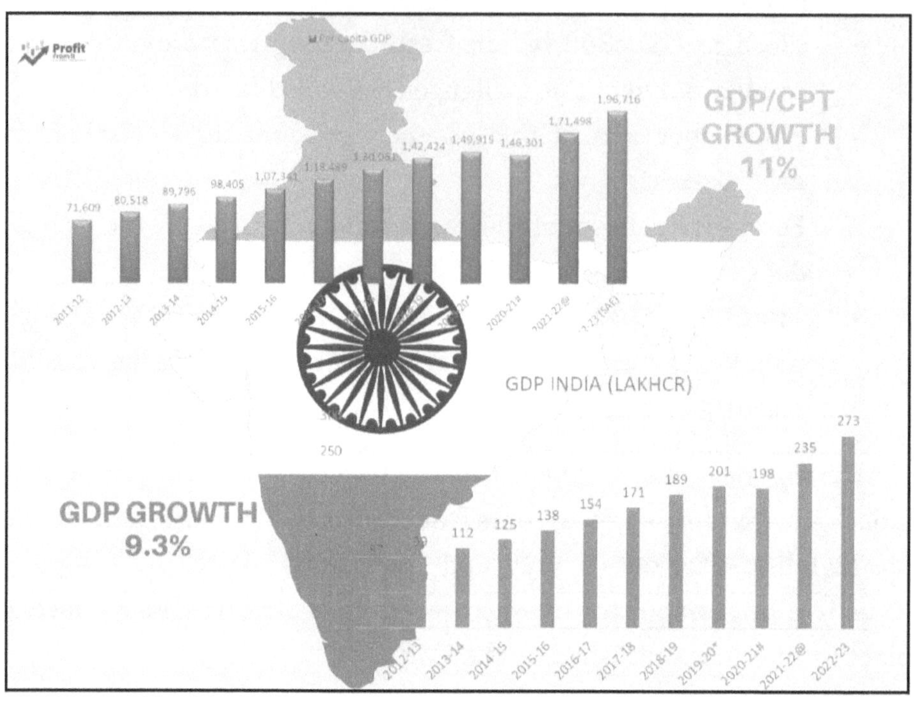

Challenges Ahead!

Since 2020, we saw three dark events which affected the world economy drastically. The world saw Covid-19, which had a harsh effect on the economy leading to a de-growth in GDP worldwide. As the world was just recovering from the first dark event, we saw a geopolitical crisis in the Russia-Ukraine war. This created a trade disruption worldwide and the commodity prices started shooting up. After decades of stability, the world witnessed a staggering inflation. Both poor countries and advanced economies were greatly affected. To curb the inflation, central banks raised the interest rates, which interrupted the growth of many countries. The rising interest rates, coupled with the rising inflation, made people cautious, as they were paying substantially more for the same old products. Consequently, they began consuming less, and discretionary products were largely affected.

Inflation and interest rates also hurt the profits of companies as the cost to run business increases. Hence, the profits margins decrease. This affects the overall yield of investors. Generally, during such times, large corrections are seen in the market. We can see in the chart below how the US inflation hit a four-decade high last year.

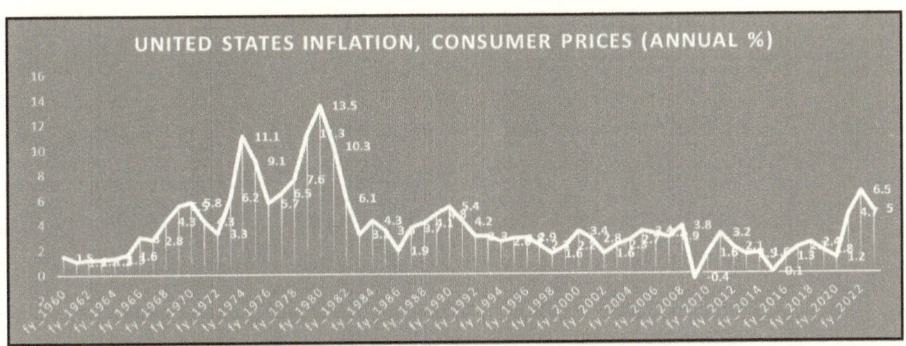

Hence, since last year, we have seen corrections in the stock markets globally. Most commodities, including base metals, crude oil, food prices, fertilizer, natural gas and coal prices were on the rise. Even during this challenging time, India stood much better than other countries in terms of GDP, inflation, interest rates and other factors.

- We saw FPI Equity outflows from most of the developing economies during these trying times. Amidst all this, India was still better placed even if we compare the general debt to GDP ratio change for major economies during the years 2005–2021. Japan, with 175% government debt in 2005, is at 263% today. Even the US, which was at a highly comfortable 66% in 2005, is at 128% today. India only saw a minor change. In 2005 it was 81%, and today, it is at a highly comfortable 84%. This is a clear achievement for India as depicted in the chart below.

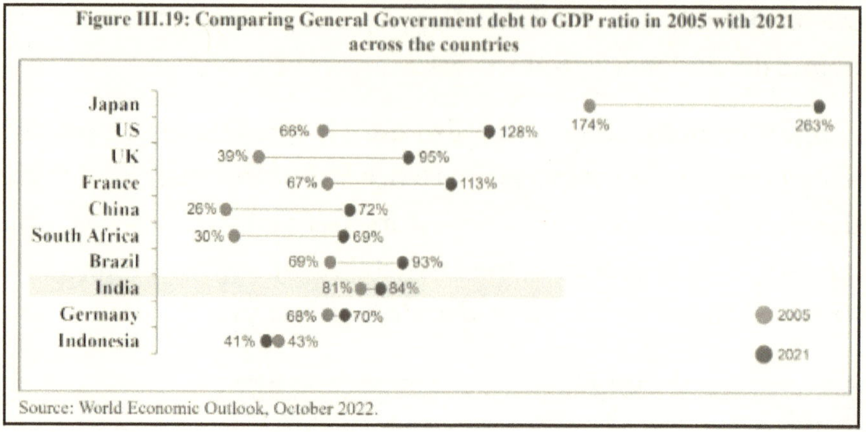

Source: World Economic Outlook, October 2022.

- The core debt of major economies except India is higher than what it was in 2008. The core debt for the US, China, Japan, Germany, the UK and India has risen by 33%, 155%, 122%, 3%, 34% and (–7%), respectively. This shows how India has outperformed its peer countries during the past year, setting the stage for further growth in the coming years.

- The GNPA, which was of concern to the banking industry in India, has now gone down, and is again at a comfortable level. This also sets the stage for banks to offer new credits.

- The median age of India stands at 30, making it the youngest major economy. India is going to stay the youngest among major economies for the next few decades. This sets the stage for India's high productivity.

Combining many such growth parameters, it is estimated that India will be the fastest growing major economy in the 21st century. Despite challenges, we have already improved our GDP ranking from 15 in 1995 to 9 in 2010. In 2015, India jumped to the 7th place. Currently, India is ranked 5th, moving ahead of our master, the UK, along with France. It is estimated that India will become the third largest economy by 2030, overtaking Germany and Japan. India's leap to success has been charted below.

world GDP

RANKING	Year 1995	Year 2010	Year 2015	Year 2023	Year 2025	Year 2030
1	United States	United States	United States	United States	United States	China
2	Japan	China	China	China	China	United States
3	Germany	Japan	Japan	Japan	Japan	India
4	France	Germany	Germany	Germany	Germany	Japan
5	United Kingdom	France	Kingdom	India	India	Germany
6	Italy	Kingdom	France	United Kingdom	Kingdom	United Kingdom
7	Brazil	Brazil	India	France	France	France
8	China	Italy	Italy	Italy	Canada	Canada
9	Spain	India	Brazil	Canada	Italy	Italy
10	Canada	Canada	Canada	Korea, Rep.	Korea, Rep.	Korea, Rep.
11	Korea, Rep.	Federation	Korea, Rep.	Brazil	Australia	Australia
12	Netherlands	Spain	Federation	Australia	Federation	Spain
13	Russian Federation	Australia	Australia	Federation	Brazil	Indonesia
14	Australia	Korea, Rep.	Spain	Spain	Spain	Russian Federation
15	India	Mexico	Mexico	Mexico	Indonesia	Mexico

Yes, get ready for India. '*Aapna time vapas aa gaya hai.*' It's India's time now. The country has entered its *Amrutkal* and there are big promises as we move closer to 2047, when the country will celebrate its 100th year of Independence. We must jump to the number one position by 2047.

Marketcap and GDP

Market capitalization, sometimes referred to as marketcap, is the total value of a publicly traded company's outstanding common shares owned by stockholders. Market capitalization is equal to the market price per common share multiplied by the number of common shares outstanding.

Marketcap grows well when GDP growth is good, and it remains sluggish when the GDP is sluggish. However, there are some instances when the marketcap has not grown despite a growing GDP. This is entirely possible. But when does this happen? This happens when inflation is high or when interest rates increase. This is because the marketcap has a co-relation to the profitability of the listed companies; the profits of these companies decrease when inflation and interest rates are high. Hence, the marketcap does not grow during such times. However, generally speaking, if the GDP grows, the marketcap will also grow. This is evident from the below example.

Here we can see that the world GDP growth was high during the 20th century and hence the marketcap growth was also high. The GDP grew by 8% during the years 1975–2000. Hence, the marketcap grew even higher by 14% during the same period. Whereas, if we see GDP growth during the 21st century, it is at just 5%. Consequently, the marketcap growth during this century is sluggish at just 5%. Yes, we can say the marketcap responds to the GDP growth. The higher the growth, the better the return in the market.

If we look at the same parameters for India, our market cap used to remain at a discount for a long time. When India's GDP in 2000 was close to USD 0.5 trillion, our marketcap was USD 0.23 trillion. As the GDP grew over time, it hit USD 1.4 trillion in 2009, USD 2.5 trillion in 2015 and USD 2.9 trillion in 2019, respectively. Similarly, the marketcap also grew to USD 1.4 trillion in 2009, USD 1.8 trillion in 2015 and USD 2.3 trillion in 2019, respectively. Today, we can proudly say that our GDP and marketcap have reached USD 3.4 trillion even as I write this book. We can say that our GDP and marketcap is Rs. 270 lakh crores. It is estimated that by 2030, India may reach a GDP of USD 7.2 trillion. Hence, our marketcap can also reach more than USD 7.2 trillion, approaching close to USD 9 trillion. We can expect India's marketcap to remain at a premium due to high investor confidence in the world's largest democratic nation. Observe the clear correlation between GDP and marketcap in the figure below.

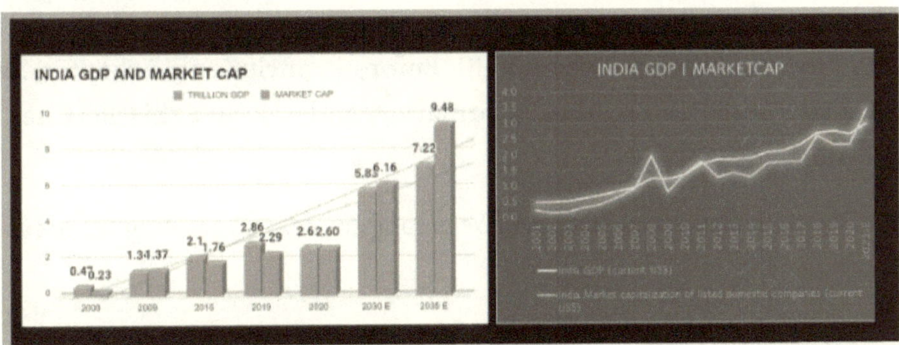

We may also notice many similarities to China's growth, as we saw during the last 30 years. The GDP of China in 2007 was USD 3.6 trillion and that of India was similar. China's GDP grew to USD 7.6 trillion by 2011, that is, in the span of four years. India's GDP may also grow similarly to USD 7.8 trillion in the next eight years. China's GDP/ capita was as low as USD 2,700 in 2007 and increased to USD 5,600 in 2011. Making a similar projection, India's current GDP/capita which is USD 2,600, may rise to USD 5,200 in the next eight years. This is explained very well in the Morgan Stanley report. For further clarity, let me share the chart from their report.

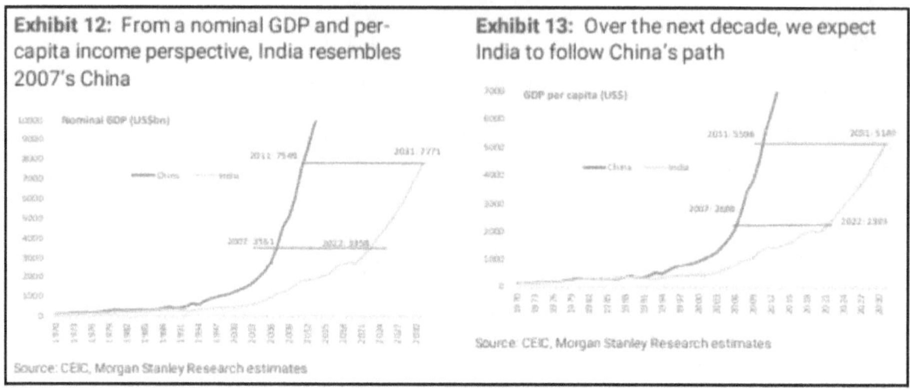

The current marketcap in terms of rupees in India is exactly Rs. 275 lakh crores. Soon you may see newspaper headlines even before this book gets published, stating that India's marketcap has crossed the landmark of Rs. 300 lakh crores. So let me congratulate you all in advance. Similarly, we can anticipate crossing the landmark Rs. 500 lakh crore marketcap before 2030. Before I conclude this chapter, let me share some interesting information and ask you this pertinent question:

Do you believe that India will be among the fastest growing economies in the world?

Then, my friend, you are most welcome to invest in India.

Now, let me directly talk about Nifty rather than the marketcap.

- When the GDP was USD 0.5 trillion, Nifty was 1,000 just 20 years ago.
- When the GDP reached USD 1.5 trillion, Nifty was at 6,000 just a decade ago.
- When the GDP reached USD 3 trillion, Nifty was at 17,000 just 3 years ago.

Now the question is:

Where will you estimate Nifty to be if by 2030 India's GDP touches USD 7 trillion?

The answer gives me goosebumps, just imagining the potential of future investments. If you agree that our country is ready for the quantum leap, then let's get ready to take the next step. If you agree that India offers unlimited investment opportunities for the future, then it's time to explore the growth engines.

The next step of this exercise is to look out for these precious investment opportunities. Should you blindly pour our money into stock markets, or would you rather pick and select those Indian industries which are booming and some new emerging sectors waiting to outperform in the future? Should you not investigate and analyze these sectors which are the engines for our current economic growth and search out those which we think have the greatest potential for future growth?

Not surprisingly, we are bound to come across many industries which are lagging. These are companies which are available at cheap prices, because they are not able to capture the demand. You must identify these companies, too, so that you can clearly keep away from bad investments. Investment in these companies can disturb your planning. You need to be cautious with these types of sectors, so that you don't sink your precious funds. What do you think? Is it worth spending time and effort on studying the industries and sectors which command maximum demand? Get ready for a very interesting discussion.

Demanding Industries: Look Out for Sectors with High Demand in the Booming Economy

> National progress is the sum of individual industry,
> energy, and uprightness, as national decay is of individual
> idleness, selfishness, and vice
>
> **– Samuel Smiles**

In any country, there can be innumerable types of industries. The classification of industries can vary depending on the criteria used, but here are some common categories:

- Manufacturing industry: This sector involves the production of goods ranging from automobiles and electronics to textiles and food products.

- Service industry: Service-based industries focus on providing various services, such as banking, healthcare, education, hospitality, transportation, telecommunications, and professional services like legal and accounting.

- Agriculture and farming industry: This industry includes activities related to cultivation, farming, livestock, fisheries, forestry and other agricultural practices.

- Mining and extraction industry: This sector involves extracting natural resources from the earth, including minerals, metals, oil, gas and coal.

- Construction industry: This sector encompasses building and infrastructure development, including residential, commercial and public projects.
- Financial industry: This industry includes banking, insurance, investment firms, asset management and other financial services.
- Information technology (IT) and software industry: This sector focuses on software development, hardware manufacturing, IT services, telecommunications, and technology-related products.
- Healthcare industry: This industry covers healthcare services, including hospitals, clinics, pharmaceuticals, medical equipment manufacturing, biotechnology and research.
- Energy industry: This sector involves the production, distribution, and supply of energy resources, including oil, gas, electricity, renewable energy sources, and utilities.
- Retail industry: This industry encompasses the sale of consumer goods through various channels, such as physical stores, e-commerce, and wholesale distribution.
- Transportation and logistics industry: This sector includes transportation services (air, land, and sea), logistics management, shipping, warehousing and supply chain operations.
- Media and entertainment industry: This industry covers broadcasting, film production, television, publishing, advertising, digital media, gaming, and other entertainment-related activities.
- Automotive industry: This sector focuses on the manufacturing, distribution and sales of automobiles, motorcycles and related components.
- Aerospace and defence industry: This industry involves the production of aircraft, spacecraft, defence equipment, weapons and related technologies.

- Education industry: This sector includes educational institutions, training centres, e-learning platforms, educational publishing and educational technology companies.

Note that this list is not exhaustive, and there can be additional subcategories or specialized industries within each sector. Industries may vary in prominence and size depending on the country's economic structure, resources and development stage.

Industries can be classified using various criteria based on their characteristics and activities. Here are some common methods of classifying industries:

1. *Economic sector classification*: Based on this, industries can be classified as primary, secondary and tertiary sectors.

    a. Primary sector: This sector includes industries involved in the extraction and production of raw materials, such as agriculture, mining, forestry and fishing. Before the Industrial Revolution, this was the sector which contributed the most to the GDP. As the world learned to produce, the next sector came into significance.

    b. Secondary sector: The secondary sector encompasses industries that transform raw materials into finished goods through manufacturing and construction activities. This sector bloomed post the Industrial Revolution, as we learned to make textiles from cotton, manufacture steel from ore, etc. Companies in this sector started growing large in and around the 20th century. Even the second Industrial Revolution gave a boost to this sector, as we learned to mass produce goods. As the world started to earn more, the need of a third sector arose and now this is the sector which contributes most to the GDP. This sector came to be known as the tertiary sector.

    c. Tertiary Sector: This sector comprises industries that provide services to individuals and businesses, such as banking, healthcare, transportation, retail and education. Today, this is the largest sector. The Third and Fourth Industrial Revolutions are from this sector.

As investors, we should recognize that the tertiary sector is the most recent sector, and the highest growth is seen in this sector. Meanwhile, the primary sector is bound to slow down a bit and grow less than the secondary and tertiary sectors.

We may classify industries based on the product or output.

2. *Product or output classification*: Industries can be classified based on the type of products or outputs they produce. For example:

- Manufacturing industries: Industries involved in the production of physical goods like automobiles, electronics, textiles and food products.
- Service industries: Industries that provide various services, such as banking, healthcare, hospitality, telecommunications and professional services.
- Extractive industries: Industries engaged in the extraction of natural resources, including mining, oil and gas, and forestry.

Industries can also be classified based on technology.

3. *Technological classification*: Industries can be classified based on the level of technology and innovation involved in their operations. For example:

    a. High-tech industries: Industries that involve advanced technology, innovation and research, such as information technology, biotechnology and aerospace. GPS, space and drone technology are also a part of this industry.

b. Low-tech industries: Industries that rely on basic technology and traditional methods, such as agriculture, textiles and some manufacturing sectors.

The next classification is based on ownership. How?

4. *Ownership and control classification*: Industries can also be classified based on ownership and control structures. For example:

a. Public-sector industries: Industries owned and operated by the government, such as public utilities, defence and some healthcare services.

b. Private-sector industries: Industries owned and operated by private individuals or companies, including most manufacturing, services and retail sectors.

c. Non-profit or voluntary sector: Industries involved in charitable, educational, social and community services.

These are just a few classification methods, and industries can be categorized in various ways depending on the purpose and context of the classification. It's important to note that industries may overlap or fall into multiple categories based on their activities and characteristics.

Apart from classification, it is important for an investor to know how industries grow.

Industries go through various phases of growth and transformation as they evolve over time. Although the specific trajectory can vary depending on factors like industry type, market conditions and technological advancements, here is a general framework of how industries move through different phases of their life cycle.

- **Introduction phase:** In this phase, a new industry emerges, often driven by innovation or a change in market demand. New products, services or technologies are introduced, and initial players enter the market. The industry may face challenges in establishing itself, creating awareness and gaining market acceptance. This is when stakeholders need to invest more and more and cannot expect a high return immediately. This is the investment phase. The industry may stay for some time in this phase before it moves on to the next phase.

- **Growth phase:** Once the industry gains traction and the products or services are accepted, it enters a period of growth. The demand for the products or services increases, attracting more participants, including new entrants and investors. Existing players expand their operations and production capacity to meet the growing demand. This phase is characterized by rapid revenue and market share growth. Yes, this is the time of strong growth. Profits start flowing but substantial investment may be needed to expand. This is when the industry enters the next stage.

- **Maturity phase:** As the industry matures, the pace of growth slows down. Market saturation is reached, and competition intensifies. Established companies focus on improving efficiency, reducing costs and innovation to maintain their market position. Consolidation may occur through mergers and acquisitions, and barriers to entry may increase. The industry reaches a stable state where growth rates level off. This is when stakeholders receive the maximum rewards. Initially, stakeholders invest money in the company, and it is at this stage that they reap the rewards, with continuous and consistent earnings. All these cycles are long. It may take several decades to transform from one stage to another.

- **Decline or transformation phase:** Industries may face a decline if their products or services become outdated or face strong competition from substitutes or disruptive technologies – just as the smartphone replaced old telephones and cameras, and digital media is replacing print media. We can even see OTT platforms eating into the market share of multiplexes. However, a decline can also be an opportunity for transformation and rejuvenation. Companies within the industry may need to adapt and innovate to meet changing customer preferences and market dynamics. This phase may involve diversification, adopting new technologies or entering new markets to revive growth.

Disruption and emergence of new industries: Some industries may experience disruptive changes that render existing business models obsolete. Technological advancements, shifts in consumer behaviour or regulatory changes can pave the way for the emergence of new industries. Disruptive industries often offer innovative products or services and redefine market dynamics, leading to the decline or transformation of existing industries.

It's important to note that not all industries follow this exact sequence, and the duration of each phase can vary significantly. Additionally, industries can experience cycles of growth and decline, depending on various external factors. Flexibility, adaptability, innovation and the ability to anticipate and respond to market changes are crucial for industries to successfully navigate these phases and sustain long-term growth.

Growth in industries is seen due to different aspects including penetration, affordability, reach, new products, technological advancements, regional spread and inorganic growth. Industries can also grow by dipping into the market share of the unorganized sector. For example, the retail sector was largely unorganized; now we see organized retail in the form of department stores, EBOs and MBOs.

Just to illustrate how industries grow, the restaurant industry in 2014 was valued at Rs. 2.7 lakh crore, where 30% of the market was unorganized. Today, the market has grown to Rs. 5.5 lakh crore, where 45% of the market share is held by the organized sector. So, the real growth of the restaurant industry is just 11%, but the organized sector has grown by 16% and within this organized sector, the chain restaurants have grown by 20%. So, investment in chain restaurants can provide high growth. Right?

Companies like Zomato, Policybazar and Byju's fall under the emerging industries, where substantial investment is still needed to expand and gain market share. We can say that restaurants, labs, banking, and insurance are some examples of growing industries. Companies like HUL, Nestle and TCS can be classified as mature industries and hence they pay back more to stakeholders.

What can we say about the paint industry which has been in existence since pre-Independence? There were several players like Shalimar, Asian, Berger, Kansai and many more. The paint industry today is valued close to Rs. 1 lakh crore. Will this industry grow more or are we going to see decay? Let's take a closer look.

The paint industry 10 years ago was just a Rs. 30,000 crore industry, while today it has grown to Rs. 1 lakh crore. We can expect this industry to grow well in the future. Why?

- The per capita consumption of paint in India is just 4.1 kg/capita, which is relatively low when compared with the global average of 14 kg/capita. China consumes 7.2 kg/capita. So as income grows, this gap is going to close.

- Until now, 33% of the market is with the unorganized sector. Post-GST we saw the organized market in India gaining a share in different industries. The paint industry was also benefited by this move. Companies grow in two ways: The first growth comes from increasing consumption and the second growth comes by eating into the pie of the unorganized sector. In addition, as income grows, people tend to opt for brands.
- Here there are two types of markets. The first is the fresh market, which involves the first-time painting of new properties. The second market is larger, as this is the re-paint market. So, the market increases both ways. The repainting frequency increases as income grows. Till 2010, people used to undertake repairs every eight years; now this has come down to five years. This boosts the sales of paint companies.
- Urbanization and nuclearization of families have helped the market grow.
- Housing for all (PMAY) and smart cities are also going to help.

So, from the above example of the paint industry, we saw how the industry grew and this immensely helped the companies belonging to this sector. For example, Asian Paints, the largest company, with 43% of the total market share, has grown from a Rs. 1,500 crore turnover during FY2003 to a Rs. 35,000 crore turnover in FY2023 – a 20X growth in 20 years. Such growth helps investors create huge wealth. How?

When Asian Paints turnover was Rs. 1,500 crores, their profits were Rs. 140 crores. If you invested a 1% stake in this company, your profit will be Rs. 1.4 crore. As their turnover grew to Rs.35,000 crores, their profits grew to Rs. 4,200 crores. Hence, your profit of Rs. 1.4 crore with 1% stake, has increased to Rs. 42 crores. If you had made this investment 20 years ago, the total dividends received today is equal to the amount invested. Just try and guess how long you will continue to receive dividends on this one-time investment? As long as Indians continue to paint their houses. Infinity! This is wealth! Who helped create this wealth? Asian Paints. Who helped Asian Paints grow? The paint industry.

Hence, it is important to look for growing industries that can consistently grow. The paint industry is an example of a secondary industry which has been in existence for a long time. There are many other new age industries. Below are examples of industries in different phases:

Emerging industries:

a. Electric vehicles (EVs): With the increasing focus on sustainable transportation, the EV industry is rapidly emerging, driven by advancements in battery technology, government incentives and growing environmental awareness.

b. Virtual reality (VR) and augmented reality (AR): These industries are still in their early stages but are showing significant potential across various sectors, including gaming, entertainment, education and healthcare.

Growing industries:

a. Renewable energy: The renewable energy industry, including solar and wind power, is experiencing a significant growth due to the increasing demand for clean energy sources and government support for sustainable initiatives.

b. E-commerce: With the rise of online shopping, the e-commerce industry continues to expand, driven by technological advancements, convenience and changing consumer preferences.

Mature industries:

a. Automobiles: The automobile industry has reached a mature stage, with well-established players and intense competition. Companies focus on improving existing models, technological advancements (such as electric vehicles) and expanding into new markets. They are well penetrated.

b. Telecommunications: The telecommunications industry has matured, with widespread connectivity and established players. The focus now lies on expanding infrastructure, improving network capabilities and offering innovative services.

Decaying industries:

a. Film photography: With the advent of digital photography, film photography has experienced a decline. The industry has significantly contracted, with fewer players and limited market demand.

b. Physical media: Industries related to physical media, such as CDs, DVDs and physical books, have faced a decline due to the rise of digital streaming, e-books and online platforms.

It's important to note that the classification of industries into these phases is not static, and industries can transition between phases or exhibit characteristics of multiple phases based on market dynamics, technological advancements and other factors.

We have also seen some of the old giant conglomerates of India transform from primary market players in the early years, to secondary and now tertiary industries, all in pursuit of growth.

Initially, the Tatas invested in the tea and coffee business, but they also invested in manufacturing like Tata Steel, Chemical and Tata Motors, and now they are big in IT, with companies such as TCS. Today, their largest profitability comes from tertiary industries.

Similarly, Reliance was for the most part in oil refineries in the early years, but today they are the no#1 player in retail and telecommunication. What could be the reason? Growth is the answer.

We saw the Mahindra group enter the steel industry and they moved on to tractors. Now they have M&M Finance, Tech Mahindra and Mahindra Holidays.

These are some examples of how giant corporations are also on the lookout for demanding and growing industries.

Wealth is there where there is growth.

Can we consider the below listed industries to be growing industries?

- Banking
- Defence
- Consumer electronics
- Airline
- Cement
- Insurance
- Technology
- Travel and tourism
- Breweries

Yes, why not?

The country's Ministry of Commerce and Industry regularly publishes some indicators which can tell us if there is growth in a particular industry or not. They are known as high frequency indicators as they reflect the economic activity of particular sectors.

High-frequency indicators are economic data points that provide real-time or frequent updates on the current state of an economy. These indicators are useful for tracking vital economic activity and can provide insights into short-term trends. While the exact set of high frequency indicators can vary depending on the country and the available data, here are some examples commonly used in GDP analysis:

Industrial production index: This data in India is provided on the 12th of every month. This index measures the output of the manufacturing, mining and utilities sectors. It indicates the level of production and can provide insights into the overall health of the industrial sector.

Retail sales: Retail sales data tracks the total sales of goods and services by retail establishments. It reflects consumer spending patterns and can indicate the strength of domestic consumption. This data is provided in GDP updates published every quarter.

Purchasing managers' index (PMI): The PMI is a survey-based indicator that measures the economic health of the manufacturing and services sectors. It provides information on factors such as new orders, employment and production levels.

Trade data: Trade data includes exports and imports of goods and services. Monitoring trade figures helps assess the level of international trade and can indicate the external demand for a country's products. This data is provided every month.

Jobless claims: Jobless claims or unemployment data tracks the number of individuals filing for unemployment benefits. It provides insights into the labour market conditions and can indicate changes in employment levels.

Housing starts: Housing starts data measures the number of new residential construction projects initiated during the period. It provides an indication of the strength of the housing market and can reflect consumer confidence and investment in the real estate sector.

Consumer confidence index: The consumer confidence index measures consumer sentiment regarding the overall state of the economy and their personal financial situation. It can influence consumer spending behaviour.

Vehicle sales: Provided the first week of every month, vehicle sales data tracks the number of new vehicle registrations or sales. It provides insights into consumer demand and can reflect trends in the automotive industry.

These high-frequency indicators, along with other economic data, are used to analyze short-term economic trends, assess business cycle fluctuations and make informed policy decisions. They offer more frequent updates compared to quarterly or annual GDP figures, enabling policymakers and analysts to have a more current view of the economy.

Pre-liberalization industries were mainly government oriented with fewer jobs and opportunities. Hence, even the top Indian companies were from the public sector.

For example:

- SAIL was not only the largest steel company, but it was among the largest in Nifty-50 pre-1991.
- MTNL: The largest telecom player was in Nifty's Top 5.
- LIC: The largest insurance company
- SBI: The largest bank was in Nifty's Top 5
- ACC: Among the largest companies in 1936.
- Bombay Dyeing: Among the largest textile companies in Nifty.

See the pre-1991 adverts, when Licence Raj was in force. We had to wait long to buy even a car or anything new through the pre-booking system. And look at today's world of advertising. We are in the 'Instant

Gratification Zamana'. Today, it's easy to buy a car and bike immediately with credit that is readily available.

The pre-1991 era was known as Licence Raj. The term 'Licence Raj' refers to the system of extensive government regulations and licensing requirements that were in place in India prior to the economic liberalization reforms of the early 1990s. Under the Licence Raj, businesses had to obtain licences and approvals from various government agencies for almost every aspect of their operations. These licences were required for setting up new businesses, expanding existing ones, importing and exporting goods, obtaining raw materials, and even determining the production levels and pricing of goods. The government controlled the allocation of resources, determined investment priorities and had a significant say in economic decision-making.

Thus, the creation of jobs was within the power of a few hands. Hence, jobs were in high demand due to fewer opportunities. Markets were not open and were controlled by a few MNCs and PSUs. Hence, GDP growth was low and per capita income was at its lowest.

Following the economic liberalization reforms in India in the early 1990s, the country experienced a significant acceleration in industrial growth. The reforms dismantled many of the regulations and barriers that had previously stifled the Indian economy, leading to increased investment, healthy competition and productivity. Several industries witnessed rapid growth and transformation as a result of these reforms. Here are a few notable examples:

Information technology (IT) and software services: The IT industry in India experienced an exponential growth post-liberalization. The availability of a skilled English-speaking workforce, cost competitiveness and the relaxation of restrictions on foreign investment and technology imports contributed to the emergence of India as a global IT and software services hub. Companies like Tata Consultancy Services (TCS), Infosys, Wipro, HCL Tech and Tech Mahindra replaced many slow growth companies and industries from Nifty-50, and they became major players in the global IT outsourcing market. Today, TCS and Infosys are among the largest employers in India. TCS, with 6 lakh+ well-paid employees, leads the GDP/capita growth. Similar patterns were seen in many industries at that time.

Telecom and mobile services: The liberalization reforms led to the opening of the telecommunications sector to private players. This led to a rapid expansion of mobile and telecom services across the country. Companies like Bharti Airtel, Vodafone Idea and Reliance Communications played a crucial role in transforming India's telecom landscape and increasing mobile penetration. Today, Reliance JIO has emerged as the major player with around 45 crore users, followed by Bharti Airtel. Due to this, India has been able to lead the technology in the communication sector.

Automobiles: The liberalization reforms brought in foreign investment and technology in the automobile sector. International car manufacturers established their presence in India, leading to the growth of the automobile industry. Domestic companies like Tata Motors and Mahindra & Mahindra also expanded their operations and introduced new models. The automobile sector became a major contributor to India's manufacturing output and exports. Today, both Tata Motors & M&M are in the Nifty-50, along with a few major two-wheeler companies.

Banking and financial services: The liberalization reforms paved the way for the entry of private banks and foreign banks into the Indian market. It increased competition and innovation in the banking sector. Additionally, the establishment of the National Stock Exchange (NSE) and the Securities and Exchange Board of India (SEBI) facilitated the growth of the capital markets and improved the scope and safety in investment opportunities. We saw the emergence of banks like HDFC Bank, ICICI Bank and Kotak Bank, which took the lead and were featured among Nifty-50s top 15 performers. HDFC Bank is India's third largest company by marketcap and has the largest marketcap in the banking industry. It is among the country's top employers.

Pharmaceuticals: Liberalization allowed Indian pharmaceutical companies to tap into global markets and benefit from increased foreign investment. India became one of the largest producers and exporters of generic drugs worldwide. Companies like SunPharma, Cipla, Dr. Reddy's Laboratories, Divis Lab and many others became prominent players in the global pharmaceutical industry. They too secured their place in Nifty-50.

These are just a few examples of the industries that experienced rapid growth post liberalization in India. The list includes companies in many other industries also. The economic reforms created opportunities for entrepreneurship, innovation and competition across various sectors, leading to increased industrial growth, and contributing to India's emergence as one of the world's fastest-growing economies.

We saw companies grow abundantly. Here are some examples:

- HDFC bank, which emerged during the private banking boom, rose from just a Rs. 2,000 crore turnover company during the beginning of the 21st century, to a company with a turnover of more than Rs. 2 lakh crores today.
- TCS, which emerged during the IT boom, rose from a Rs. 2,000 crore turnover company during the beginning of the 21st century, to a company with a turnover of more than Rs. 2 lakh crores today.
- RIL, which was just in oil, later diversified into different growing industries like retail and telecom and benefited from this boom, rising from just a Rs. 2,000 crore turnover company during the beginning of the 21st century, to a company with a turnover of Rs. 7 lakh crores today, becoming the largest company in sales, profit and marketcap.
- LT, the largest construction and engineering company, saw strong growth, going from a Rs. 8,000 crore turnover during the beginning of the 21st century, to a turnover of almost Rs. 2 lakh crores.
- Asian Paints, the largest paint company, saw strong growth, going from a turnover of just Rs. 1,000 crores during the beginning of the 21st century, to a turnover of close to Rs. 35,000 crores.

Due to this post-liberalization growth in India, we witnessed many wealth generating companies which have grown tremendously along with strong corporate governance.

At the same time, we saw a spike in the number of small companies. India's entrepreneurs are no longer dependent on government jobs. Many companies have witnessed gigantic growth depending on the sectors they operate in. Many business houses who were initially in a different industry made use of this growth, diversifying into growing industries. This has helped India grow its per capita income.

What if India had continued with the Licence Raj scenario and not pursued privatization and economic liberalization? Several scenarios would likely have emerged:

Slow economic growth: The Licence Raj system was characterized by excessive government control, bureaucracy and restrictions on businesses. This would have hindered economic growth and development. The lack of competition, innovation and investment would have limited productivity and stifled entrepreneurship. India would have struggled to achieve sustained high growth rates and the standard of living would not have improved.

Limited foreign investment: The Licence Raj discouraged foreign investment due to its restrictive policies and barriers to entry. Without privatization and liberalization, India would have continued to face challenges in attracting foreign capital. This would have limited access to advanced technologies, capital inflows and international collaboration.

Lack of industrial modernization: The Licence Raj often favoured established industries and discouraged new entrants. This would have hindered industrial modernization and technological advancements. Without competition and market forces, industries would have had little incentive to innovate, upgrade technology and improve efficiency. As a result, India's industries would have lagged global standards.

Inefficient resource allocation: The Licence Raj system involved government control over resource allocation, including raw materials, licences and permits. This would have led to inefficient allocation of resources, with political considerations and corruption playing a significant role. Scarce resources would have been misallocated, and industries would have faced challenges in obtaining necessary inputs.

Lack of consumer choice and quality: The Licence Raj limited competition and discouraged the entry of new players in various sectors. This would have resulted in limited consumer choice and poor quality of products and services. The absence of market forces would have reduced incentives for companies to improve product quality, innovate and meet consumer demands effectively.

High corruption and red tape: The Licence Raj system was notorious for corruption, bureaucracy and red tape. The complex and discretionary nature of licences and permits would have perpetuated a culture of corruption. This would have undermined governance, eroded public trust and hindered efficient administration.

It is important to note that the economic liberalization and privatization reforms in India have been instrumental in transforming the country's economy and contributing to its growth in recent decades. These reforms have opened new avenues for investment, increased healthy competition, improved efficiency, and expanded opportunities for entrepreneurship and innovation.

The balance of payment crisis which India faced in 1991 was also due to this mismanagement. As we recovered from this crisis through proper reforms, India's real hidden potential started to shine.

Moving ahead, let us see how industries capture their market space.

Industries grow over time as the awareness about a particular product or service increases. Later, they start penetrating their market space. We see industries grow in two ways. First, they increase the number of users and volumes, and secondly, over time, price appreciation is achieved.

Just to illustrate the point:

PARTICULAR	Price in1991	Price in 2021	Growth
Rice	2.3	19.4	8.4X
Milk	5.5	48	8.7X
USD	19.9	73.4	4.1X
Petrol	14.6	101.8	7X
Washing machine	7,290	10,990	1.5X
Maruti car	167,000	329,835	2X
Refrigerator	6,800	10,000	1.5X
Soft drink	4.5	20	4.4
Cooking gas	67.9	834.5	12.3X
Air ticket (DEL–MUM)	1,800	2,466	1.4X

If the prices increase in the same fashion exponentially, then how on earth are we going to live the life? Are we forgetting to consider something important here?

If the prices of products and services have increased over time, so has our individual incomes. Let us see how.

Particular	Price in 1991	Price in 2021	Growth
Per capita income	583	12,140	20.8X
Peon's salary	750	18,000	24X
Cabinet secretary fees	30,000	2.5 lakh	8.3X
CEO (Avg. Top)	65 lakhs	64 crores	99X
Cricketer/match	9,000	15 lakhs	167X

The above table shows that our income grew more than the prices.

As our incomes grew, we exited the 'Necessity Based' economy and entered the 'Discretionary Spending' economy. Increased income helps companies grow more. It allows them to launch premium products also. When 45% of the Indian population was below the poverty line pre-liberalization, companies selling goods and services were highly affected as the consuming population was smaller with a lower ticket size. We could not expect companies like Voltas, that sells ACs, to penetrate the market like in other countries. For example:

- Cement: The average Chinese uses 2,000 kg/year versus the 220 kgs consumed by Indians.
- Clothes: The average Chinese spends five times more than an Indian.

Why do they consume more than us? Because their income is five times more than ours. Why is their income five times more than ours if they were like us in 1980? Because they took steps towards economic development 20 years ahead of us.

Today, if our GDP is Rs. 272 lakh crores, the listed companies account for around Rs. 150 lakh crores. There are around 179 sectors (it increases every year) listed under the Bombay Stock Exchange currently. Out of the total sectors, 20% of them contribute to 80% of the total market capitalization. What does this indicate? This data gives us a very important clue.

A study of the sectoral data was an eye-opener for me! I understood that for our money to grow big and create wealth, we should invest only in industries where there is growth! Most people are satisfied with a little profit here and there and very few investors have the patience to sieve out the huge wealth creators and stay invested in these growth sectors with a long-term investor mindset.

Just imagine the change we are seeing today. The top eight companies before 2000 were ONGC, IOCL, HINDUNILVR, SAIL, MTNL, SBI, RELIND, and Tata Steel. You can see that most of them were public sector units as there were no incentives for privatization. The combined profits of all these companies at that time was Rs. 15,000 crores. If you look at today's top eight companies, each company individually makes more than the combined profits of the top eight at that time. So, the companies that did not grow have been replaced with those that have shown good growth.

To understand which sectors are growing in a particular country, you can follow these steps:

Research economic indicators: This data is provided monthly and quarterly by various Ministries. Start by researching and analyzing key economic indicators of the country, such as GDP growth rate (every quarter), employment rate (monthly), inflation rate (monthly), and foreign direct investment (FDI) inflows (monthly). These indicators can provide a broad overview of the country's economic performance and indicate sectors that are experiencing growth. For example, if we check GDP data quarterly, we can clearly identify the growth of different industries. Even monthly IIP data provides growth data of industries, both in the goods and services sectors. For example, if we study the GDP data, we can ascertain if the economy is growing or not. This will reflect in the results announced by companies, and we can observe price movements. GDP is an advance indicator. Similarly, inflation data, which is made available monthly, tells you in advance whether your companies are going to make profits or not. These are advance indicators.

Study government policies: Examine the government policies and initiatives in the country. Governments often prioritize certain sectors for development and growth through policies, incentives and reforms. Look for sectors that receive government support, investment and regulatory reforms, as they are likely to exhibit growth potential. For example, the government announced, 'Make in India', 'Buy from India', and huge capex spending for the defence sector. What does this suggest? This indicates that defence companies will experience growth. Similarly, NIP (National Infra Pipeline) was announced with Rs. 100 lakh crores infra spending in the next five years. What does this mean? Yes, we know it's good for the infra sector. We saw the PLI scheme for many manufacturing companies, and we know it's good for the manufacturing sector. We saw the *'Naal Se jal'* yojana. This can boost sales of the plastic pipes industries. There's a focus on tourism. What does this suggest? You know the answer, right?

Analyze industry reports: Consult industry reports and market research studies that focus on the country's economy. These reports often provide detailed insights into specific sectors, including their growth prospects, investment trends and market dynamics. They can help you identify sectors with significant growth potential and emerging trends. Many research companies and government institutes provide such reports.

Track investment and funding trends: Monitor investment and funding trends within the country. Observe where venture capital, private equity and foreign investments are flowing. Sectors attracting substantial investments are typically experiencing growth and garnering investor confidence.

Stay updated on technological advancements: Keep track of technological advancements and innovation trends within the country. Technological disruptions often lead to the emergence of new sectors and drive growth in existing sectors. Monitor advancements in areas such as artificial intelligence, biotechnology, renewable energy and digital transformation, as they can create opportunities for growth. OTT platforms, drone technology, food delivery are just a few of the many areas that you should keep track of closely.

Monitor consumer behaviour and demographics: Understand the changing consumer behaviour and demographics of the country. Analyze consumer spending patterns, lifestyle preferences and evolving needs. This information can help identify sectors that cater to changing consumer demands and have the potential for growth.

Network and engage with industry experts: Attend industry conferences, seminars and investment or networking events. Engage with experts, professionals and the leading thinkers in various sectors. Conversations with industry insiders can provide valuable insights into growth sectors, emerging opportunities and challenges.

By combining these steps and conducting thorough research, you can gain a better understanding of which sectors are growing in a particular country and make informed decisions regarding investments, business opportunities or career choices.

The source I relied upon to identify demanding industries was BSEIndia. I studied the results on the BSEIndia website, which was easy to understand. Increasing sales is a clear indication of demand, while decreasing or low growth in sales is a clear indication of muted or decaying growth.

Checking the growth of some of the responsible companies can give you insights. Let us take a closer look at long-term, mid-term and short-term growth.

Understanding long-term, mid-term and short-term growth is essential for developing effective strategies and making informed decisions in various areas such as business, investments and personal goals. Here's a breakdown of each term and how to understand them:

Long-term growth:

Long-term growth refers to sustained and significant progress over an extended period, typically spanning several years or more. More than 10-, 15 – or 20-years growth is generally considered to be long-term growth.

Analyzing trends: Examine historical data, market trends and industry forecasts to identify patterns and potential growth opportunities.

Mid-term growth:

Mid-term growth falls between short-term and long-term growth, typically covering a period of three to less than 10 years.

Short-term growth:

Short-term growth focuses on the immediate timeframe and can span from current quarterly growth up to a three-year timeframe. It suggests what is happening right now. Is the industry growing or facing challenges? Short-term growth study can answer this question.

You should invest in those industries where growth is visible. Once you are able to observe the past growth based on historical data, check its mid-term and short-term growth to understand its mid and short-term behaviour.

Here are some of the current inputs on industries to predict future growth, from where you can learn to predict the future of different industries:

1. RHP: Whenever a company comes out with its IPO (Initial Public Offering) they have the detailed research material called Red Herring Prospectus. The column 'Industry Overview' will help you understand the industry in which the company

operates. I have studied the behaviour of different industries from the RHP.

2. Annual Report: This report includes the column 'Management Discussion' which will give you several insights into the industry.

Both the above-mentioned reports are valuable reports, which can teach you many things needed for long-term wealth creation. You should be able to predict the average growth expected in any industry. Your industry should at least provide you 1X to 2X of GDP growth. If you can identify the industry that will give you this growth, most of the work for wealth creation is done.

Remember, these terms may vary depending on the context and industry. It's crucial to adapt and tailor the understanding of growth timelines as the more the industry grows, the higher the probability of wealth creation.

Market forces:

The words 'demand' and 'supply' have a special connection with all kinds of markets. They are the keywords to the development of varied groups of sectors and industries around the world. Demand can be associated with various words including necessity, wants, desires, dreams or just plain requirements. Call it what you may, but it draws you like a magnet. It is the most important thing that occupies your mind and life.

Demand is the basic energy that moves all kinds of businesses. Thousands of years ago, it was the same demand for gold and metals, which made the miners dig the earth. It was demand for food that led people to hunt in the forests, harvest the lands and plough the fields. It made them sail their ships and trawl the seas. But back then, life was simple. It was mainly connected to the earth and its

resources. The primary sectors grew initially and ruled the world in those days. Even today, the primary sectors meet the demand for basic commodities like metals, grains, energy and fuel.

After a few centuries, agrarian life changed. New demands came into being. Creativity bloomed and newer varieties of products made from the primary resources came into the sphere. Higher efficiency, productivity and skills were needed to feed this demand, and as it bloomed, the number of hands to make these products fell short. Machines were needed. It was the beginning of a new era – the industrial era. **Construction and manufacturing** became the buzz word for success. Electricity was invented. Simple machines were invented and everything new from watches to bridges, from automobiles, ships and planes, fertilizers to food products were no longer made through hard toil and sweat in the fields, but by swift machines. Seeing this huge business opportunity and the ever-increasing demand for products, entrepreneurs invested their funds into these sectors to manufacture and sell automobiles, pharmaceuticals, food products, textiles, fertilizers, chemicals and many other retail products. Mechanized products were bought and sold everywhere. *Industrialize or perish* – the great words of Sir M. Vishveshwaraiah, was the slogan of the time. Organized business systems were formed to raise money and invest in these **secondary** demanding sectors. Many inventions were made including the telegraph, telephone and electricity. They lit up the world. Anything was possible! Man even went to the moon!

Even today, the products from the secondary sector continue to witness ever-increasing demand. Some industries in this segment are able to command good margins, while many others earn low margins due to high raw-material costs, high debt, high attrition and the cyclical nature of business, etc.

The massive change in production capacity and the growing demand for newer and more sophisticated products changed business models and family structures too. The evolving face of economics and social life created a subsequent demand, and it grew in equal measure. Somebody needed to support the industries and their businesses to keep the books in order, so the accountant entered the picture. He gave them his services. Subsequently, someone was needed to look after the money, so the banking system grew. These developments necessitated other services including security, marketing, legal issues, healthcare, education, nursing and childcare, to support all this economic activity. Working people did not have time to do everything themselves. This saw the birth of the **service sectors** or **tertiary sectors**. Banks, universities, hospitals, legal firms and a variety of other professionals cropped up to support this new demand.

As time flew, technologies improved and information technology, digital technology, logistics, recruitment, travel, ticketing, entertainment, tourism, retail and so many specialized services took over. They united the various cultures, nations, peoples and geographies. Global services and specialized technologies became possible all at once. More than 60% of the GDP comes from the service sector today.

The latest trend is the **quaternary – knowledge sector.** Ruled by research and development, education, artificial intelligence, training, etc., this sector is constantly evolving and giving birth to new surprises.

Currently, words like fast food, instant access, swift delivery, cloud kitchens, quick installation, direct delivery, etc., are trending. This new sector is a mix of the service sector and high-tech development of the manufacturing sector. It involves data and internet, cashless transactions, e-learning, e-banking, domain ownership, R&D, AI, virtual realities and many more. This new fast-paced demand is changing the face of humanity. It is changing the way we live and interact in society.

In the 1950s, most of the population was dependant on agriculture. This sector's contribution to the world GDP was more than 50%. The contribution of the industrial and service sectors was not very significant at that time. By 2010, the service sectors overtook both industry and agriculture.

The point to note from the above narrative is that society has invested in so many different sectors over time and everything was based on the existing demand. When things changed gradually the older sectors became less fancy and took a back seat. Yet, a few companies from the old sectors remained evergreen because they were willing to change their approach and upgrade themselves through better research and technology. Out of all these sectors, who took the biggest booty home? Who created business empires? Who made the decisions to diversify, change and grow consistently for decades? There are several interesting examples of success and failure that we can study.

So how can we say that a particular industry is in demand?

An industry is in high demand when it experiences strong and sustained growth, increased consumer interest and increased demand for its products or services. Here are some indicators that can suggest a high demand for an industry.

Growing market size: The industry's market size expands over time, indicating an increasing customer base and demand for its products or services. There will be an increase in the volume of products. For instance, the auto industry was witnessing a strong growth, but post 2017, the volume of auto vehicles failed to increase.

What does this suggest? The demand was low. Low volume will eventually lead to low sales revenue. We saw a muted growth in many major auto companies between 2017 and 2021. The telecom market was penetrated, and the number of users did not increase post 2017. What does this mean? We saw many companies like Idea Vodafone making huge losses due to decreasing sales and increasing costs. If the number of department stores or restaurants or even bank accounts increase, what does this suggest? This increment in volume or number of users will eventually reflect in the revenue.

Increased sales and revenue: The industry is experiencing a consistent and significant increase in sales and revenue, reflecting a high demand for its offerings. If your products or services are growing faster than the country's growth (GDP growth) we can say that the product or service is in good demand.

Shortage of supply: If there is a shortage of supply relative to the demand, such as long wait times or backorders, it indicates a high demand for the industry's products or services. Sometimes, it even indicates a mismatch in the supply side of raw materials.

Rising prices: When prices for goods or services in the industry are increasing due to high demand, it suggests strong consumer interest and a willingness to pay higher prices. Reliance Jio was offered for free; today we pay 180/month. Why? Demand has been created. Zomato used to offer free delivery services. Today, they charge Rs. 20 or even more. Why do people pay? The demand has been created.

High employment and job opportunities: The industry creates a significant number of job opportunities and witnesses increased employment due to the demand for its products or services. We saw increased employment in the IT and banking sectors during the last two decades. This indicates the huge demand for the services these companies offered. Contrarily, we are seeing layoffs in developed countries in the IT industry; it suggests a slowdown in the short term.

Positive industry outlook: Market research reports, expert opinions and industry forecasts project a growth outlook for the industry, indicating a high demand in the future. High-capacity utilization for certain sectors also reflect the high demand.

Innovations and technological advancements: The industry witnesses innovations, new product developments and technological advancements, suggesting a response to high market demand and the need for improved offerings.

It's important to note that high demand in an industry can be influenced by various factors, including economic conditions (increasing income of Indians), consumer preferences (people's choices change with more money in the pocket), market trends, technological advancements (how many times do you stand in the queue now to print your passbook in the bank?), and government policies (offering benefits to local manufacturers). Additionally, demand can vary between different industry sectors, products or services.

Evaluating these indicators and considering the context of the specific industry will help determine if an industry is in high demand. Market research reports, industry analysis and expert insights can provide valuable information to assess the demand levels within a particular industry.

How I track demand: I track the volumes data and sales data of top contributing listed companies in different sectors. For example, if there are 100 listed companies in a particular sector and the top 20 companies are responsible for 80% of the sales (we generally see this in 80% of the sectors), I track their volumes. E.g.: The number of vehicles sold in case of auto companies, pairs of footwear sold by footwear companies, the credit demand in banking, or the premium sold by insurance companies. It is a good indicator to check how the industry is growing. It is not necessary to check all 100 companies as 80% of the turnover comes from the top 20 companies. These are the companies responsible for a substantial portion of the sales in the industry. I track the revenue growth for the current year (to identify current trends), for five years (to ascertain mid-term growth) and even for 10 to 20 years as it reflects consistency and long-term growth. Initially, I was surprised to find that those sectors which showcased growth were the very sectors that housed the wealth creating companies. So, sectors are more important than companies. If a sector is strong, companies are strong; if a sector is weak, companies also become weak.

The increasing number of restaurants and food-order trend helped the restaurant industry grow. Hence, Jubilant Foods was able to increase sales drastically. The slowdown of the auto industry had a negative impact on Maruti between 2017 and 2022. Post 2022, as the auto industry started picking up, companies like Maruti and Tata Motors got back on the growth track.

Smart businessmen are always on the lookout for demanding and emerging sectors to invest in and make their empires grow. We too can learn from them. Take the Tatas, for example. They initially invested in the metal sector with steel (Tata Steel). They also invested in the chemicals sector, again a primary industry (Tata Chemicals). Later, they saw the growing demand for IT services and entered the IT sector by creating Tata Consultancy Services. Today, TCS is the biggest IT firm in India, and is the largest contributor to the Tata group. The Tata group did not stop there. Recognizing the growth and potential of the IT field and its constant innovation, they diversified their business further into Tata Elxsi. They understood the potential of retail and launched Trent, Titan, etc. Studying the potential growth in demand in the food and beverages sector, they started Tata Global

Beverages. Recently, they invested and re-entered the Airlines Sector – an old passion of the great legend Mr. JRD Tata – by taking over Air India.

A study of the investing pattern of the Reliance Group, the Adani Group, and the Mahindra & Mahindra Group shows us that expansion and diversification is a great way to keep abreast of the changing times. Being diversified helps us to participate in the various stages of growth and the life cycle of businesses. The stronger sectors act as shock absorbers and allow us some leeway to make a few mistakes because no one can be right all the time. Some decisions are bound to go wrong, and all sectors may not perform well all the time.

For example, Reliance Industries was the blue-chip of yesteryears and is the Number One even today. Why? Because from their initial entry into the energy sector, they steadily diversified their business into emerging demanding sectors like the retail and digital industry. They changed their focus from decaying industries to demanding industries. Meanwhile, some of the companies which were in the Top 100 industries in 2007, are not in the forefront today. This includes ONGC, NTPC, and IOC, among others. Can you guess why? Even though they are quality companies with profitable businesses and give consistent dividend, they belong to the old industrial sectors of primary or secondary industries like energy, telecom, PSUs, etc. Their demand has stagnated, and growth and margins have slowed down. Today, people forget the old names like Bombay Dyeing and many others which were in the Nifty-50. These companies did not recognize the changes in industry, and so today, they themselves have lost their sheen.

Change is of essence and every few years the economic scenario throws up new opportunities. We need to focus on the upcoming industries also, to have a good mix in our portfolio.

> *If you resist change you resist life*
>
> **– Sadguru**

As an investor, I must check out the growing industries regularly. But some caution is required here. We cannot say that every emerging business is going to be profitable. One must study the data and put in some homework before diving in blindly. Every now and again, we see a new sector blooming in the markets. But is it safe to just jump into the bloom and market frenzy of any one single sector? Take, for instance, the renewable energy boom, the tech bubble and many other frantic booms. Hordes of investors carelessly bought every company in these sectors by only tracking the price charts. In the frenzy and excitement, nobody had time to do a proper study of the fundamentals and the features of the sector. After a while, the bubble burst and along with it many dreams crashed! The hard-earned savings of innumerable innocent investors vanished. It was a big lesson learned. A serious investor must make a note of the subtle developments that emerge, keeping track of the results of the company.

Listed companies on the Main Board must declare their annual and quarterly results regularly (there are some exemptions for SMEs). Read the annual reports, attend those conference calls and collect investor information. Track the quarterly growth. Most people track only price movements, charts, indicators and easily get swayed by negative and positive news, making swift buy and sell decisions. With repeated wasteful activity, we disturb and destroy our portfolio.

Let us see how the blue chips of today came into the limelight:

The growth factor has moved away from the primary and secondary sectors to the service and tertiary sectors, but are you still sitting on a pile of industries from those sectors where growth has slowed down? Textiles, paper, fertilizer, mining, energy, realty, etc., were in the Nifty-50 at one time. Companies from these sectors, like IOC, Vedl, DLF, BPCL and NMDC, are no longer a part of Nifty-50. They have been replaced by new entrants.

In 1986, ACC was on the top of the chart in Sensex 30 and today it is in the BSE 100.

Observe the changes and understand that reforms and other significant developments provide a growth platform for new entrants from time to time.

What is your estimate? Which companies can grow in 2030? In the next few years, we anticipate that India will move towards becoming a 10 trillion economy. Our journey from a developing to developed nation has already begun! What could be the impact of this progress in terms of growth and demand in the different industries we invest in? Just let me ask you some basic questions which can help you identify some demanding industries. Are you ready?

- If India's GDP is to grow from the current USD 3.2 trillion to USD 8 trillion by 2032, which industries are going to grow along with the GDP? Just take your time and try to build a list of sectors. Can you identify a few? Let me ask you a few more questions.
- If India's GDP/capita grows from the current 1.96 lakh to 5 lakh this decade, which industry will grow? Will consumption increase? Will discretionary spending increase? Will insurance and investment increase? Continue with your own list.
- If households with an annual income exceeding Rs. 28 lakhs grow from the current 56 lakhs to 2.5 crores, which industry

will witness a boom? Will packaged foods, out-of-home dining, restaurants, tourism and premiumization in consumption and discretionary spending boom?

- If the retail market is going to grow from the current Rs. 63 lakh crores to Rs. 150 lakh crores, which sectors are going to grow? Will consumption increase? Will apparels and accessories grow? Will departmental store and e-commerce companies grow their sales?

- If credit to GDP grows from the current 57% to 100% this decade, which sectors will witness a boom? Will finance companies or banking grow?

- If IT exports grows from the current Rs.15 lakh crores this decade to Rs. 42 lakh crores, which sector will benefit? Will the software industry benefit or not? What about IT-enabled services?

Can we expect the current Rs. 250 lakh crore market capitalization to reach Rs. 1,000 lakh crores this decade itself? I have no doubt!

Just think about it. Where is the 45% of the population which languished below the poverty line today? If we assume that this figure reduces to 5%, then don't you think 40% of the population will turn into a huge consuming machine? Multinational companies know this and hence India is on track regarding its growth plan. Amazon, Microsoft, Google, Apple, Tesla, Uber and many more have the 'India Plan' on their priority investment list.

Do you have your 'India Plan' or not?

If we have witnessed the boom in the banking and finance sectors today, we should accept that in 1991, the credit market was just Rs. 2 lakh crores. Today, it is Rs. 127 lakh crores and we already have companies with sales of more than Rs.1 lakh crores. What if the same credit market reaches Rs 300 lakh crores this decade? Can we not assume that India will have at least five companies with more than Rs 2 lakh crores in sales? This is too conservative. We will definitely have more.

Considering the 'Make in India' campaign with benefits like the PLI scheme, and reforms like *Gatishakti* to reduce the internal transport time, should we not be optimistic about the boom in manufacturing companies? We missed the golden opportunity to grow in the 20th century, but not this time around. This is India's century, and our time has come. This decade, we may see double digit growth in the export of goods, an area where we had lacked expertise.

We saw strong growth during the last 20 years due to privatization. In the next 30 years, India is going to transform from a developing economy to a developed economy. From being a low-income country to a high-income country. Are you ready, not only to benefit but also to contribute? India needs each of you to contribute and generations from now will remember you. Yes, you!

- It is assumed that by the end of this decade, around 39% of the population of India will be in the rich or higher income slab.
- The internet and connectivity are going to narrow the gap between rural and urban income.
- We may see 65% internet penetration, which could help internet-related industries to grow well.
- Online shoppers will grow from 18 crores to 45 crores, which is equal to the US population. Just imagine the online transactions Indian consumers will be conducting with different companies sitting in the comfort of their homes.
- GST has already formalized the Indian market. We will see organized market share grow well in different sectors like food, retail or even paints and ceramics.

- India is currently a rural country. Huge urbanization is going to happen this decade. This will boost the housing industry, home furnishings, smart transportation like the metro or bullet train and the airline industry?

- The median age of India is around 29 years and India is going to stay the youngest major economy for the next few decades. What will be the spending habits of this youthful population? Branded products or services may gain a bigger market share. Think about it. Young India will need around 10 crore jobs. Which sector will provide placements? Young India will get married; we may see around 10 crore marriages this decade. Which sectors will receive a boost from these marriages?

What wonderful opportunities you can avail in Incredible India! If you cannot successfully invest in India, then where should you go? You live in a country with abundant opportunities.

> *Most people overestimate what they can do in one year and underestimate what they can do in ten years*
>
> **– Bill Gates**

From the sectors listed on the stock exchanges, don't you think we can search out at least 50 such sectors where there has been consistent demand historically, and where there is going to be continuous growth in sales, profits and market share in the coming years. Don't memorize the name of the companies, memorize the names of the sectors. If you stay with growing sectors you are going to earn.

As we discussed in the previous step, India's GDP is now USD 3.2 trillion and is fast moving towards USD 7.9 trillion by 2030. Our marketcap is estimated to grow from USD 3.5 trillion to USD 10 trillion during the same period. This works out to three times the current value. So, with Nifty at 17,000 currently, what do you expect Nifty to be in 2030. Simply put, it is going to be three times the current value, right? Won't it be worthwhile to check which sectors are going to participate in this high jump to success?

STEP 4

Top Quality Companies: Search for Top Quality Companies from Demanding Industries which Can Grow and Give Consistent Income

> It's far better to buy a wonderful company at a fair price, than a fair company at a wonderful price
>
> **– Warren Buffet**

Purpose: Search for quality companies. This means you need to see whether the profits of companies you plan to invest in are also growing along with sales. Consistent profits can give lifelong passive income from investments. Don't invest in low quality companies that give inconsistent dividends.

Investing in quality companies is generally considered a prudent strategy for long-term wealth creation for several reasons:

- **Strong fundamentals:** Quality companies typically exhibit strong financials, including solid revenue growth, healthy profit margins and a robust balance sheet. These companies often have a history of consistent earnings and a proven track record of success, indicating their ability to weather economic downturns and deliver sustainable long-term returns.

- **Competitive advantage:** Quality companies often possess a competitive advantage or a unique value proposition that sets them apart from their peers. This advantage can be in the form of superior technology, strong brand recognition, a large customer base or intellectual property rights. Such companies are better positioned to withstand market fluctuations and maintain their market share over time.

- **Stability and resilience:** Quality companies tend to be more resilient during economic downturns or market volatility. Their strong fundamentals and competitive advantage provide a level of stability that allows them to navigate challenging times better than weaker or less-established companies. They may also have the financial strength to invest in research and development, innovation or strategic acquisitions to further strengthen their position.

- **Dividends and growth potential:** Quality companies often generate consistent cash flows, enabling them to pay regular dividends to shareholders. These dividends can provide a steady income stream for investors and enhance long-term returns. Additionally, quality companies have the potential for capital appreciation as their business grows and their stock price increases over time.

- **Lower risk:** Investing in quality companies generally involves lower risk compared to investing in lower-quality or speculative companies. While no investment is entirely risk-free, quality companies typically have a more stable business model, reduced debt levels and better governance practices. This can help mitigate potential downside risks and protect investors' capital in the long run.

It is important to note that investing in quality companies does not guarantee profits or eliminate all risks. Market conditions, industry dynamics and other factors can still impact the performance of even the highest-quality companies. Therefore, thorough research, diversification and a long-term investment perspective are crucial for successful wealth creation.

We know how challenging it can be for new investors to identify growing industries and select the right companies that are progressing consistently within the growing sector. A proper study is crucial to identify which companies can give multi-year rallies and provide a consistent source of funds over the years. We must dive deeper to pick out only the top-quality companies from within the growing sectors because just growth in sales and volumes are not good enough to last long if the company does not pass the quality tests.

We should never forget this formula:

No Growth Sector + Top Quality Companies = No Wealth and Appreciation: We only get dividend incomes that are consistent, but the business does not grow. So, we receive passive income that does not grow. Take NMDC, for example. There is no sales growth, hence the company gives regular dividends, but there's no appreciation.

Growth Sector + No Quality = Companies in this sector may grow and as a result the price may appreciate due to growth, but there will be less consistency in profit-making. As a result, we receive some passive income that is highly volatile. For example, the company Future Retail witnessed huge growth but it lacked quality, and the debt burden was high. Even though sales grew tremendously, it didn't convert to profits. Thus, there was no wealth creation.

Growth Sector + Quality Companies = This will provide consistent passive income that grows over time. Wealth is created from companies like Dmart rather than from debt burdened companies like Future Retail. Why? Dmart boasts quality and growth.

In the previous chapter, we understood what growth sectors are. In this chapter we will go through the quality parameters.

From our study of growing industries in the previous chapter, we recognized some industries where there is continuous demand and so their businesses have a good inflow of revenues. We also saw some big conglomerates like the Tatas and Reliance that are constantly expanding and diversifying their operations in growing sectors. We even identified some sectors that are emerging and some that are in the de-growth phase.

In our stock selection process, **growth** is the first requirement. Most importantly, there must be demand and that demand should be growing at a good Cumulative Average Growth Rate (CAGR), better than the growth rate of our GDP at current prices. So why should growth be more than the GDP at the current price and not the constant price? What is the difference?

GDP at constant prices and GDP at current prices are two different measures used to assess the economic output of a country, but they are calculated using different approaches.

- **GDP at Constant Prices (Real GDP):** GDP at constant prices, also known as real GDP, considers the changes in the prices of goods and services over time by using a fixed base year as a reference. It measures the value of all final goods and services produced within a country's borders using constant prices from a specific base year. By removing the effects of price changes, real GDP provides a more accurate picture of the underlying changes in production volume or output. Real GDP is useful for analyzing economic growth and comparing output across different time periods. It allows investors to isolate the impact of changes in production levels, technology, and efficiency, separate from the influence of inflation or deflation. Real GDP growth rates provide a measure of how much the economy has expanded or contracted after adjusting for price changes.

- **GDP at Current Prices (Nominal GDP):** GDP at current prices, also known as nominal GDP, calculates the value of all final goods and services produced within a country's borders using the prices that prevailed in the year of production. It reflects both changes in production volumes and changes in prices, including inflation or deflation. Nominal GDP represents the current market value of the goods and services produced in a given year. Nominal GDP is useful for understanding the total monetary value of economic output and the size of an economy. It is commonly used for comparing the economic output of different countries or regions at a specific point in time. However, nominal GDP figures can be distorted by changes in prices, making it difficult to assess the true changes in production levels over time.

To summarize, GDP at constant prices (real GDP) adjusts for changes in prices, allowing for meaningful comparisons of production levels over time. GDP at current prices (nominal GDP) reflects both changes in production and changes in prices, providing a measure of the total monetary value of economic output.

For example, if Maruti sold 11.7 lakh cars in FY2013 and during the FY2023 they sold around 19.7 lakh cars, we can say that unit sales grew by 5%. But the companies are smart. They generally increase the price of products or services every year. In reality, Maruti's revenues were Rs. 29,600 crores in 2010 from the total of 10.2 lakh cars sold, while in 2023 they earned a revenue of Rs. 1.18 lakh crores from a total of. 19.7 lakh cars sold. By achieving 5% CAGR growth in car sales, they were able to achieve a revenue growth of 10%! Amazing! How is this possible? Their real growth is 5%, but still they achieved 10% growth. How can this be? Because they systematically increased prices along the way. This is just like inflation.

To invest in the stock market, we should see that our industry or company value grows more than the nominal GDP and not the real GDP.

Growing demand creates natural tailwinds for all companies doing business in the same sector. Most companies in that growing sector generally perform well. Does this mean that every company from a growing sector is a top-quality company? Can we invest in all the companies from this one growing sector? Not at all! It will be too risky to do that.

Say, for instance, you have identified that the private banking industry will give 15% CAGR growth in future. To begin, we must start screening some strong company from the private banking industry. During the last 15 years we saw that the advances of private banks grew from Rs 5.2 lakh crores to Rs 45.6 lakh crores. This is a very good growth rate of 16.7%, This suggests that our investment in this industry may produce a 16.7% return. Right or wrong?

Let's assume you invested in IDBI Bank 15 years ago. A strong growth in advances helped IDBI bank also to grow. Advances of Rs. 82,000 crores in FY2008 has now become Rs. 1.5 lakh crores, which is a mere 4% growth. The company failed to make consistent profits. Hence, you did not receive regular dividends and the dividends also did not grow. Your invested value of Rs 1 lakh is just Rs 64,000 today.

Despite strong growth in the banking industry your investment did not perform well enough. Let's look at one more example and you will understand the full value of this discussion soon.

Suppose you invested in HDFC Bank, and they were able to grow their advances from Rs 63,000 crores 15 years ago to 13.7 lakh crores today. This is a spectacular growth of 23% CAGR, which is better than average in the banking industry. Hence, if you invested Rs 1 lakh 15 years ago, today your value should be around Rs 13 lakhs, along with highly consistent and increasing dividends. What can you expect for the future? If the private banking industry grows, we can expect good appreciation even in future, and will receive dividends which will grow as long as people in India bank.

So, if your sector selection was right, where did you fail? Yes, company selection. You can look for several similar examples where despite strong sector selection, the investor may not have made money due to the wrong company selection. Below are some examples.

From the finance sector, if you invested in TCI Finance rather than Bajaj Finance.

From the IT industry, if invested in 3iinfo rather than TCS.

From diversified retail, if you invested in Future Retail rather than Dmart.

From the paint industry, if invested in Shalimar Paint rather than Asian Paints.

There are many, many live examples.

For wealth we need a combination of this trinity:

15–20% sales growth | 15–20% profit growth | available at fair 20 PE valuations.

Now before we discuss quality further, you need to accurately identify an industry's growth potential. Just answer the question below. You can edit your answers in the future as you get more insights on any industry.

How much sales growth can I expect in the below given industries?

1. Apparels?

2. Paints?

3. Restaurants?

4. Private banking?

5. Department stores?

6. IT consulting software industry?

7. Finance?

8. Travel and tourism?

9. Digital media?

10. Construction?

Your answers will tell you how much returns you can expect from any given industry. If you are sure that there will be a 15–20% growth in an industry, the next step is to search for top quality companies in that particular sector.

You need to search for companies that can grow their business revenues and profits consistently. What are the parameters that can help you analyze this to help you identify the best quality stocks in any sector?

There are two types of analyses for quality:

1. Quantitative analysis and

2. Qualitative analysis

What is the difference between both these analyses?

Qualitative analysis and quantitative analysis are two distinct approaches used in stock screening to evaluate and assess investment opportunities. Here's an explanation of the differences between the two:

Quantitative Analysis:

Quantitative analysis involves analyzing numerical data and using statistical models to assess a company's financial health, performance and valuation. It relies on quantitative metrics and ratios derived from financial statements, such as income statements, balance sheets, and cash flow statements. Common quantitative factors used in stock screening include:

Liquidity ratios: Profit Margin, Current Ratio, Trade Receivables, etc.

Solvency ratios: Debt-to-Equity ratio (D/E), Debt Ratio (D/R), Debt and Lease Paying Capacity or we can even call it Interest Coverage Ratio (ICR), etc.

Valuation ratios: Examples include Price-to-Earnings ratio (P/E), Price-to-Sales ratio (P/S), Price-to-Book ratio (P/B), PEG ratio (PEG), Yield, etc.

Profitability ratios: Return on Equity (ROE), Return on Capital Employed (ROCE), Return on Assets (ROA), etc.

Growth metrics: This includes metrics like revenue growth rate, Earnings per Share (EPS) growth rate, and sales growth and profit margin trends.

Dividend metrics: Metrics related to dividends, such as dividend yield and dividend growth rate.

Quantitative analysis focuses on the quantifiable aspects of a company's financial performance and uses historical data to draw conclusions about its prospects. It helps investors identify undervalued or overvalued stocks based on objective data and can be particularly useful for comparing companies within the same industry.

Qualitative Analysis:

Qualitative analysis involves assessing non-numerical information to evaluate a company's qualitative aspects, such as its competitive position, management quality, industry dynamics and growth potential. Qualitative factors are typically evaluated through subjective judgements and require more subjective interpretation. Common qualitative factors used in stock screening include:

Market share: Companies with highest market share tend to be ahead of others due to many inbuilt parameters like brand, good quality products or services, good development plans, a national player, after-sales services and many more.

Advantage: Assessing a company's unique value proposition, brand strength, intellectual property, or other factors that give it a competitive edge.

Management quality: Evaluating the competence, experience, and track record of the company's management team and their strategic decision-making.

Industry analysis: Understanding industry dynamics, competitive landscape, regulatory environment, and emerging trends that could impact the company's prospects.

Business model: Evaluating the company's business model, its sustainability, and its ability to adapt to changing market conditions.

Risk assessment: Considering potential risks and challenges that the company may face, such as technological disruptions, regulatory changes, or geopolitical factors.

Strong corporate governance: This is the quality that can take your company to the top without worries.

Qualitative analysis provides a more holistic view of a company's prospects and helps investors understand the qualitative factors that may impact its future performance. It involves gathering information from various sources, including company filings, news, industry reports, and expert opinions.

Both quantitative and qualitative analysis have their strengths and weaknesses. Combining both approaches can provide a more comprehensive understanding of a company's investment potential and help investors make informed decisions.

Let's first discuss the top parameter of qualitative analysis: Leadership. Yes, leadership is like a lion, the king of the forest.

Having the largest market share is crucial for companies as it signifies their dominance in a particular industry or sector. It brings several advantages and opportunities, including:

- **Competitive advantage:** Companies with a top market share often have a competitive edge over their rivals. They benefit from economies of scale, higher purchasing power, and greater brand recognition, allowing them to offer competitive prices and attract more customers.

- **Revenue and profitability:** A larger market share generally translates into higher revenue and profitability. Companies can leverage their market leadership position to generate more sales, negotiate better deals with suppliers and achieve greater operational efficiency.

- **Influence and control:** Dominant companies often have more influence and control over the market. They can shape industry trends, set pricing standards and dictate terms to suppliers and partners. This control further strengthens their position and protects them from potential threats.

- **Investment and partnerships:** Companies with a significant market share tend to attract more investment and partnership opportunities. Investors and potential collaborators see them as stable and lucrative prospects, leading to easier access to capital, mergers, acquisitions and collaborations with other industry players.

- **Customer trust and loyalty:** High market share often reflects a strong customer base and brand loyalty. Customers tend to trust and rely on well-established companies, which reinforces the company's position and can lead to repeat purchases, customer referrals, and positive word-of-mouth.

Now, let's look at some live examples of companies with top market share in India and the US:

Indian companies:

Reliance Industries Limited (India): It holds the top market share in various sectors, including petrochemicals, refining, oil and gas exploration. Reliance Industries also dominates the Indian telecom industry. Through its subsidiary, Reliance Jio, they have the largest market share in telecom in India. Even their retail wing is the largest retail department store, seven times larger than its closest competitor.

Tata Consultancy Services (India): TCS is the largest Indian IT services company and has a significant market share in the global IT outsourcing industry. It provides a wide range of services, including software development, consulting, and business process outsourcing. They are twice as large as their closest competitor, Infosys.

US companies:

Apple Inc. (United States): Apple is known for its dominant market share in the global smartphone market with its flagship product, the iPhone. It has established a loyal customer base and consistently ranks among the top smartphone manufacturers worldwide.

Amazon.com Inc. (United States): Amazon is a dominant player in the e-commerce industry, holding a substantial market share in online retail. It has expanded its services to include cloud computing, streaming media and artificial intelligence, solidifying its position as a market leader.

Thus, we can say that a company with good leadership has top quality.

Here are a few more examples:

Page Industry is a leader in the undergarments segment, Ultratech is the reigning king in cement, HDFC Bank is the leader in private banking, Bajaj Finance leads in retail finance, Pidilite in chemicals and Wonderla in amusement parks.

Some companies command a huge market share due to the popularity and goodwill for their brand, the quality of their products, after-sales services and all the significant things that the company does to make the customer feel valuable. These things add up to create that huge market share. Small things matter and they create a big brand identity.

Companies can attain the highest market share in their respective industries due to a combination of factors. Here are some reasons, along with examples, to help illustrate this. Do remember, gaining such market share is not an easy task, it requires long-term consistency.

Product differentiation and innovation: Companies that offer unique and innovative products or services often gain a competitive advantage and capture a significant market share. They stand out from their competitors and attract customers with their distinctive features or capabilities.

Example: Tesla Inc. (United States) – Tesla is a prime example of a company that has achieved top market share in the electric vehicle (EV) industry. Its focus on cutting-edge technology, long-range capabilities and sleek design has set it apart from traditional automakers and helped it dominate the EV market.

Strong branding and customer loyalty: Building a strong brand and cultivating customer loyalty is a crucial factor in attaining top market share. Companies that consistently deliver high-quality products, exceptional customer service, and positive brand experiences tend to attract a loyal customer base, giving them an edge over competitors.

Example: Coca-Cola Company (United States) – Coca-Cola has established itself as a global leader in the beverage industry. Through decades of effective branding, marketing, and consistent product quality, Coca-Cola has secured a top market share in the carbonated soft drinks segment, supported by a loyal customer base that recognizes and trusts its brand.

Pricing and cost competitiveness: Offering competitive pricing or cost advantages can enable companies to capture a significant market share. Lower prices or cost-efficient operations can appeal to price-sensitive customers and lead to increased market penetration.

Example: Walmart Inc. (United States) – Walmart is renowned for its dominance in the retail industry. By focusing on operational efficiency, volume-based purchasing power, and a cost-effective supply chain, Walmart offers competitive prices to its customers, making it a preferred destination for affordable shopping.

Distribution network and reach: A well-established and extensive distribution network can play a vital role in capturing a significant market share. Companies with a wide distribution reach can ensure their products or services are readily available to customers, giving them a competitive advantage.

Example: Hindustan Unilever Limited (India) – Hindustan Unilever Limited (HUL) is one of India's largest consumer goods companies. It has an extensive distribution network that reaches even the most remote areas of the country. HUL's widespread presence and distribution capabilities have helped it secure a leading market share in various product categories, including personal care and household products.

Besides market share, we must also look for **good governance**. No wrong doings from the management must be tolerated and high standards of ethics and some civic responsibility is required, for a company to stand out in the long run.

An experienced management team, up-to-date technological growth and professionalism benefit in the running of a good company. We must look for these characteristics as part of the qualitative parameters of the companies we are going to choose to include in our long-term portfolio.

Let us take an example.

If we take a closer look at the leadership in the IT sector, we can identify the leading company from the below IT world:

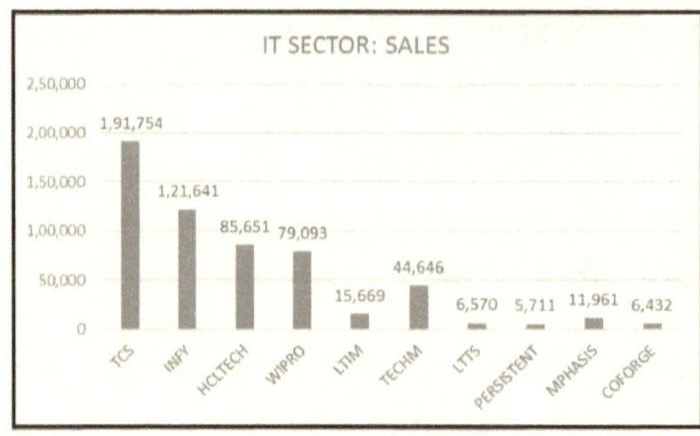

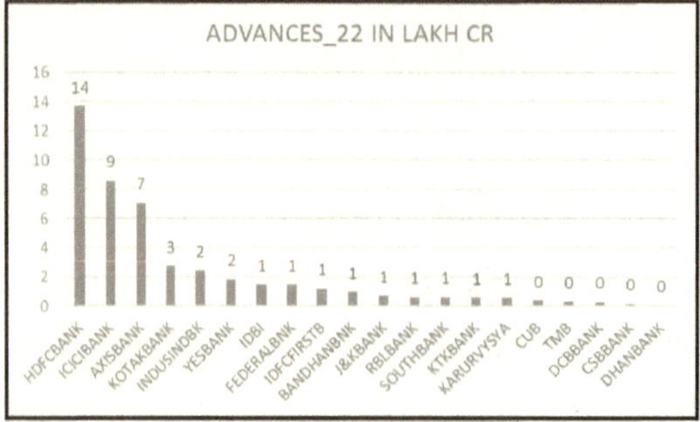

We can clearly see in the graph that TCS is maintaining the leadership in sales with high margins. Infosys is in the second position and then comes HCL, Wipro and the list goes on. We should be clear that TCS is the company responsible for maximum business.In the private banking world, the list is as follows:

You can very well see how HDFC Bank leads the advances. The second is ICICI Bank, then comes Axis, followed by Kotak, and the list goes on.

As an investor we should know the leaders in different industries.

Who has the leadership in the three-wheeler industry? As you can see, Bajaj Auto is the leader in the three-wheeler industry, with 35% market share.

Three-Wheeler OEM	APR'23	Market Share (%) APR'23
BAJAJ AUTO LTD	24,873	35.1%
PIAGGIO VEHICLES PVT LTD	5,643	8.0%
MAHINDRA GROUP	4,225	6.0%
MAHINDRA & MAHINDRA LIMITED	3,910	5.5%
MAHINDRA REVA ELECTRIC VEHICLES PVT LTD	315	0.4%
YC ELECTRIC VEHICLE	2,838	4.0%
SAERA ELECTRIC AUTO PVT LTD	1,855	2.6%
DILLI ELECTRIC AUTO PVT LTD	1,730	2.4%
ATUL AUTO LTD	1,562	2.2%
TVS MOTOR COMPANY LTD	1,128	1.6%
MINI METRO EV L.L.P	1,037	1.5%
CHAMPION POLY PLAST	987	1.4%
J. S. AUTO (P) LTD	921	1.3%
UNIQUE INTERNATIONAL	883	1.2%
HOTAGE CORPORATION INDIA	802	1.1%
Others including EV	22,444	31.64%
Total	70,928	100%

Name the leader in the PV segment?

Yes, Maruti is the leader in the PV segment with around 40% market share. Amazing, right?

PV OEM	APR'23	Market Share (%) APR'23
MARUTI SUZUKI INDIA LTD	1,09,919	38.89%
HYUNDAI MOTOR INDIA LTD	41,813	14.79%
TATA MOTORS LTD	41,374	14.64%
MAHINDRA & MAHINDRA LIMITED	29,545	10.45%
KIA MOTORS INDIA PVT LTD	16,641	5.89%
TOYOTA KIRLOSKAR MOTOR PVT LTD	13,739	4.86%
SKODA AUTO VOLKSWAGEN GROUP	6,755	2.39%
SKODA AUTO VOLKSWAGEN INDIA PVT LTD	*6,619*	*2.34%*
VOLKSWAGEN AG/INDIA PVT. LTD.	*2*	*0.00%*
AUDI AG	*134*	*0.05%*
SKODA AUTO INDIA/AS PVT LTD	*-*	*0.00%*
HONDA CARS INDIA LTD	5,572	1.97%
MG MOTOR INDIA PVT LTD	4,190	1.48%
RENAULT INDIA PVT LTD	4,156	1.47%
NISSAN MOTOR INDIA PVT LTD	2,246	0.79%
MERCEDES -BENZ GROUP	1,149	0.41%
MERCEDES-BENZ INDIA PVT LTD	*1,098*	*0.39%*
MERCEDES -BENZ AG	*50*	*0.02%*
DAIMLER AG	*1*	*0.00%*
BMW INDIA PVT LTD	866	0.31%
PCA AUTOMOBILES INDIA PVT LTD	782	0.28%
FIAT INDIA AUTOMOBILES PVT LTD	661	0.23%
FORCE MOTORS LIMITED, A FIRODIA ENTERPRISE	513	0.18%
BYD INDIA PRIVATE LIMITED	154	0.05%
JAGUAR LAND ROVER INDIA LIMITED	150	0.05%
ISUZU MOTORS INDIA PVT LTD	147	0.05%
VOLVO AUTO INDIA PVT LTD	145	0.05%
PORSCHE AG GERMANY	55	0.02%
Others	2,102	0.74%
Total	**2,82,674**	**100%**

Next, we should study the numerical performance of the companies' results, and this will give us the **quantitative parameters** with which we can measure a given reality in terms of actual numerical values and not just make vague conjectures or emotional estimates about quality. With quantitative analysis and ratio analysis, we can even compare the results between peer group companies – their performance versus other companies in similar businesses. We can compare the sales, profits and ratios. From this study we get to understand that only top-quality companies are able to convert their sales growth into profit growth consistently.

When we talk about quantitative factors, there are three aspects to consider.

1. Liquidity parameters like profit margin, current ratio, trade receivable days and a few more.

2. Solvency parameters like Debt2Equity, Debt Ratio or ICR.

3. Profitability Parameters Like ROE, ROCE, and ROA.

Another important parameter is Valuation. Valuations of a company can be got by using PE, Yield and PEG ratios. Valuation becomes important only after you have already selected a company based on its growth and quality parameters and if you are now looking for a fair value to start your investment. But for the time being, let us understand the above three quantitative parameters and then go to the valuation aspect, which will be addressed in detail in the next chapter.

Let us understand all the parameters in detail.

We will start with liquidity parameters. Under liquidity parameters, we will begin with net profit margin.

1. **Net profit margin:** Net profit margin is an important quantitative parameter that measures a company's profitability by expressing its net profit as a percentage of its revenue. It indicates how efficiently a company converts its sales into profits. Here are a few reasons why net profit margin is relevant when searching for a good company to invest in:

    a. **Profitability assessment:** Net profit margin provides insights into a company's profitability and its ability to generate earnings from its operations. A high net profit margin suggests that a company is efficient at controlling costs, managing expenses, and generating profits. It indicates that the company has a healthy business model and can generate returns for its investors.

    b. **Comparative analysis:** Net profit margin allows for the comparison of profitability across different companies within the same industry or sector. By analyzing the net profit margin of various companies, investors can identify those with superior profitability and a competitive advantage over their peers. This helps in evaluating the relative strength and performance of different investment opportunities.

c. **Sustainability and stability:** A consistent and sustainable net profit margin is an indicator of a company's stability and resilience. It reflects the company's ability to weather market fluctuations, economic downturns, and other challenges while maintaining profitability. Investors generally seek companies with a stable net profit margin, as it signifies the company's ability to generate consistent returns over the long term.

d. **Financial health:** Net profit margin is a key metric that reflects the financial health of a company. It provides insights into the company's ability to generate cash flows, service its debts, invest in growth initiatives, and distribute dividends to shareholders. A healthy net profit margin indicates that the company has the financial capacity to support its operations and sustain future growth.

e. **Investor returns:** Investing in companies with a high net profit margin can potentially result in higher investor returns. A company with a robust net profit margin has the potential to generate substantial profits, leading to increased shareholder value, dividend pay-outs, and capital appreciation. It signifies that the company can reward its investors over time.

While net profit margin is an important quantitative parameter, it should be used in conjunction with other financial and qualitative factors when evaluating investment opportunities. It's essential to consider the company's overall financial health, growth prospects, competitive position, and industry dynamics to make well-informed investment decisions.

Since all the companies from any given sector are working in the same business, we must select those smart companies in the sector who have better margins. Net profit margins of all the peer group companies from the same sector can easily be compared.

The next parameter is profit margins.

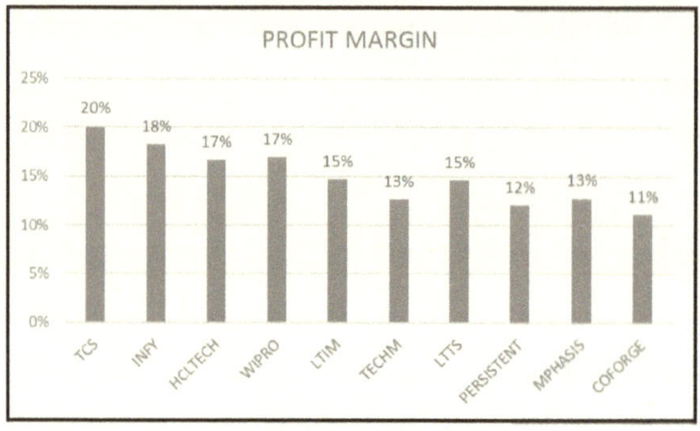

As we have already seen, TCS is the leading company in IT with the largest market share. When we look at profit margins, TCS again leads the industry with top margins. This reflects the quality of management.

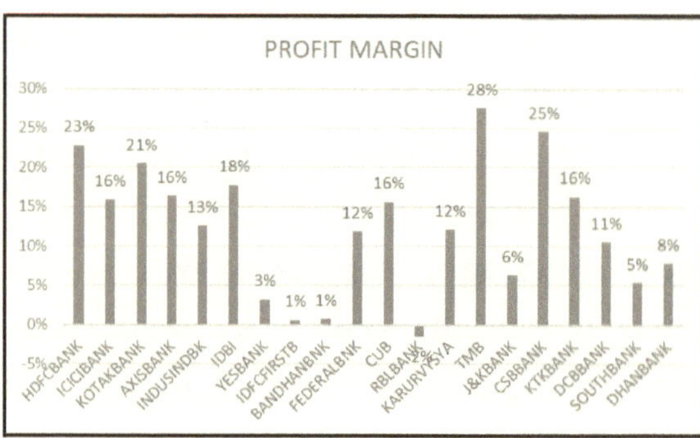

Similarly, if HDFC Bank boasted the highest advances, they are not behind when it comes to profit margins.

We can say that the company with good leadership also leads when it comes to profit margins.

High profitability provides consistent cash flow to companies and investors.

Here's the formula to calculate net profit margin:

Net Profit Margin

Net profit Margin = (Net profit / Sales) * 100

Key questions to ask: Does the company give out dividends? Does it have good reserves in the balance sheet? Can it remain profitable for long? Have the profit margins been consistently good? Note these points carefully.

After a proper study, you may observe that mature sectors generally command better margins, while emerging industries may be stressed for net profit margins in the initial years as they require funds for expansion. The key is to look for strong demand in the case of emerging sectors.

Asian Paints, HDFC Bank, TCS, and LTTS are some of the companies from high growth sectors commanding good margins and paying dividends consistently over the years. Their balance sheets also show strong reserves.

Let us move to the second indicator as regards the liquidity parameter:

The next indicator of good liquidity is the **current ratio**.

Current ratio: Current assets/current liabilities.

The current ratio is a financial metric that measures a company's ability to meet its short-term obligations using its current assets. It is calculated by dividing current assets by current liabilities. The current ratio provides insights into a company's liquidity and its capacity to cover its short-term financial obligations. Here's how it can be useful in searching for a quality company:

a. **Liquidity assessment:** The current ratio helps evaluate a company's liquidity position. A higher current ratio indicates that a company has a greater ability to meet its current liabilities with its current assets. This suggests that the company has sufficient liquidity to cover its short-term obligations, such as paying suppliers, meeting payroll, and servicing short-term debt. A quality company is expected to have a healthy current ratio, indicating sound liquidity management.

b. **Financial stability:** The current ratio is an indicator of a company's financial stability. A strong current ratio implies that the company has a solid financial footing and is less likely to face liquidity issues or default on its obligations. It demonstrates the company's ability to navigate economic downturns or unexpected challenges. A quality company should have a consistent and sustainable current ratio over time.

c. **Risk management:** The current ratio helps assess the risk associated with a company's short-term liabilities. A low current ratio may indicate a higher risk of insolvency or difficulty in meeting immediate obligations. It could suggest that the company relies heavily on short-term financing or has poor management of its working capital. A quality company should maintain a current ratio that provides a comfortable cushion to mitigate liquidity risks.

d. **Comparability:** The current ratio allows for the comparison of liquidity across different companies or within the same industry. By analyzing the current ratios of various companies, investors can identify those with better liquidity management and risk mitigation strategies. Comparing a company's current ratio to industry benchmarks or historical performance can provide insights into its relative liquidity strength and position within the industry.

e. **Investment decision-making:** The current ratio is one of the many factors that investors consider when making investment decisions. It provides an indication of a company's ability to meet its short-term obligations and manage its working capital effectively. A quality company is expected to have a current ratio that is in line with industry standards, demonstrating a prudent approach to liquidity management.

It's important to note that the interpretation of the current ratio may vary across industries. Some industries, such as retail or manufacturing, may require higher working capital and may naturally have lower current ratios compared to others. Therefore, it is advisable to consider the specific industry dynamics and norms while analyzing the current ratio of a company.

Here are a few recent live examples of Indian companies with their current ratio (figures may change during updated new results):

Good current ratio:

Tata Consultancy Services (TCS) – current ratio: 2.44

TCS, one of India's largest IT services companies, exhibits a strong current ratio. With a current ratio of 2.44, TCS indicates a healthy liquidity position, indicating its ability to meet short-term obligations comfortably.

Hindustan Unilever Limited (HUL) – current ratio: 1.38

HUL, a leading consumer goods company in India, maintains a solid current ratio of 1.38. This indicates that HUL has sufficient current assets to cover its current liabilities, suggesting good liquidity management.

Bad current ratio:

Vodafone Idea Limited – current ratio: 0.70

Vodafone Idea, a major telecom operator in India, has faced financial challenges in recent years. With a current ratio of 0.70, it indicates a relatively weaker liquidity position, potentially implying difficulties in meeting short-term obligations.

Reliance Infrastructure Limited – current ratio: 0.70

Reliance Infrastructure, an infrastructure development and construction company, has a current ratio of 0.70. This lower current ratio suggests a comparatively weaker liquidity position, indicating potential liquidity risks or inadequate working capital management.

After validating the leadership, quality and profit margins, you must check the current ratios of peer group companies to select the strongest.

Then comes trade receivable days which falls under the liquidity parameters.

What is trade receivable days? Trade receivable days, or DSO (days sales outstanding), is important to assess a company's ability to collect payments from its customers in a timely manner. It is more commonly used to analyze a company's performance over time or to compare it to industry benchmarks.

If you are looking for examples of companies with good trade receivables management, here are a few live examples from different industries:

Asian Paints Limited – Asian Paints is a leading paint company in India. It has demonstrated effective trade receivables management, resulting in relatively low DSO. The company's strong market position, efficient distribution network, and proactive credit control measures have contributed to timely collections and optimized cash flow. Take the latest FY2023 results: We see that trade receivables is just Rs. 4,639 crores on the annual turnover of Rs. 34,367 crores. This works out to (4,639/34,367) * 365 = 49 days. Yes, the trade receivables is just 49 days, which is efficient and better than industry standards.

Titan Company Limited – Titan is a renowned Indian consumer goods company known for its watches, jewellery, and eyewear. The company has implemented robust credit management practices, enabling it to maintain a healthy trade receivables cycle. Titan's focus on customer relationships and credit risk assessment has resulted in efficient collections and minimized credit-related risks. Take the latest FY2023 results: Trade receivables is just Rs. 674 crores on the annual turnover of Rs. 37,924 crores. This works out to (674/37,924) * 365 = 6.5 days. Yes, the trade receivables is just 6.5 days, which is efficient and better than industry standards.

Maruti Suzuki India Limited – Maruti Suzuki is a prominent automobile manufacturer in India. The company has a well-established dealer network and effective credit control policies in place. Maruti Suzuki's emphasis on timely collections, dealer management, and credit risk assessment has contributed to a streamlined trade receivables process and enhanced financial performance. Take the latest FY2023 results: Trade receivables is just Rs. 3,295 crores on the annual turnover of Rs. 1.18 lakh crores. This works out to (3,295/117,571) * 365 = 10 days. Yes, the trade receivables is just 10 days, which is efficient and better than industry standards.

However, it is not typically used to compare companies from different industries. For example, we can't compare Maruti with Asian Paints. Instead, it is more commonly used to analyze a company's performance over time or to compare it to industry benchmarks. Comparing trade receivables days across companies within an industry may not yield meaningful insights as different companies may have different customer bases, credit policies, and business models. If you compare Asian Paints with Shalimar Paints or Indigo Paints, it can give you a more accurate picture as they are all similar businesses.

We saw how net profit margins, current ratio and trade receivable days are good indicators of the liquidity of a company in the short term. Next, we should check the long-term **solvency** of the company.

Solvency ratios:

Checking solvency ratios is important while investing in companies for the long term because they provide insights into a company's ability to meet its long-term financial obligations. Solvency ratios help assess the financial health, stability, and sustainability of a company, which are crucial factors for long-term investment considerations. Here's an explanation of solvency ratios and a few live Indian company examples:

1. **Debt-to-equity ratio:** The debt-to-equity ratio measures the proportion of debt and equity financing used by a company. It indicates the level of financial leverage and the degree of risk associated with a company's capital structure. A lower debt-to-equity ratio suggests a lower financial risk and higher solvency.

   Debt-to-equity = Total Borrowings/Total equity

   Example: Tata Consultancy Services (TCS) – TCS, a leading Indian IT services company, has maintained a low debt-to-equity ratio over the years. This indicates a strong solvency position, as the company relies less on debt financing and has a sound capital structure.

   Asian Paints from the paint industry, Pidilite from the chemical industry, Titan from the gems and jewellery industry, Maruti from the passenger cars industry, Bajaj Auto from the two and three-wheeler industry and Dmart from the departmental store industry are some companies with a healthy debt-to-equity ratio. Contrastingly, PC Jeweller from the jewellery industry, Ashok Leyland, and Future Group are examples of companies with not so good debt-to-equity ratios.

2. **Interest coverage ratio:** The interest coverage ratio, in other words, the debt and lease paying capacity, assesses a company's ability to cover its interest expenses and lease liabilities with its earnings. It indicates the company's capacity to service its debt obligations and manage interest rate risks. A higher interest coverage ratio signifies better solvency and a lower risk of default.

ICR = PBITDA/Interest

Example: Hindustan Unilever Limited (HUL) – HUL, a renowned consumer goods company in India, consistently maintains a high interest coverage ratio. This indicates strong solvency and the ability to generate sufficient earnings to cover interest payments.

3. **Debt service coverage ratio:** The debt service coverage ratio evaluates a company's ability to meet its debt obligations, including principal and interest payments. It assesses the cash flow available to service debt and indicates the company's solvency and ability to honour its financial commitments.

Example: Reliance Industries Limited (RIL) – RIL, a conglomerate with interests in various sectors, has maintained a healthy debt service coverage ratio. The company's strong cash flow generation and diversified business portfolio contribute to its solvency and ability to service its debt obligations.

When considering solvency ratios, it's essential to compare them within the context of the industry and consider other qualitative and quantitative factors. Additionally, solvency ratios should be analyzed alongside other financial metrics and factors, such as profitability, cash flow generation, and growth prospects, to make informed investment decisions.

A company with unmanageable debt faces many problems. You should think twice before including such a company's stock in your long-term portfolio as too much volatility and uncertainty can spoil your planning.

For example: Ruchi Soya, Adani group, Future Group

Sales growth was good for the above companies and even the price on the charts looked good. People started buying at higher prices, but unfortunately, neither the liquidity nor the solvency ratios of these companies were right. Slowly, problems cropped up and the slightest push saw huge volatility in prices. Many innocent investors were trapped, and they suffered because they could not book out of their positions at the right time. So be cautious before you invest. I cannot stress enough how important it is to know the quality parameters of your company. During good times all companies grow, even donkeys and horses perform well, but during testing times, the true colours are revealed. Whenever the market cycles change, even the top-quality companies face volatility in their stock price, but their value remains firm because of their discipline in money management and the prices invariably bounce back.

After screening the best companies and validating their liquidity position and solvency, check their **profitability ratios**. It is a given fact that companies with good growth, favourable liquidity and solvency are bound to have good profitability. But most of us make the mistake of checking profitability ratios first and get a lopsided view that the company is good. Just profitability is not enough. It must be seen in conjunction with the other four parameters mentioned above.

Profitability ratio:

There are several types of profitability ratios used in investing to assess a company's financial performance and profitability. Here are some commonly used profitability ratios along with formulas and examples of live Indian companies:

1. **Net profit margin:** (Liquidity ratio can also be considered here)

   Net Profit Margin = (Net Profit / Revenue) * 100

   Example: HDFC Bank Limited

   Formula: (Net Profit / Revenue) * 100

   HDFC Bank's net profit margin can be calculated by dividing its net profit by revenue and multiplying it by 100.

   HDFC Bank: (45997/204,667) * 100 = 22%

2. **Return on assets (ROA):**

   Return on Assets = (Net Profit / Total Assets) * 100

   Example: Larsen & Toubro Limited

   Formula: (Net Profit / Total Assets) * 100

   Larsen & Toubro's return on assets can be calculated by dividing its net profit by total assets and multiplying this by 100.

   LT: (12624/330352) * 100 = 4%

3. **Return on equity (ROE):**

   Return on Equity = (Net Profit / Shareholders' Equity) * 100

   Example: MARUTI

   Formula: (Net Profit / Shareholders Equity) * 100

   Maruti's return on equity can be calculated by dividing its net profit by shareholders' equity and multiplying this by 100.

   Maruti: (8211/60231) * 100 = 14%

It's important to note that the formulas mentioned above provide a general understanding of how these profitability ratios are calculated. The specific financial figures used to calculate these ratios can be found in a company's financial statements, such as the income statement and balance sheet. Additionally, it's crucial to consider industry norms, trends, and other factors when analyzing profitability ratios for investment purposes.

Emerging sectors could take some time to improve their profitability ratios as they are in the development stage of their business. You can expect their profitability to improve along with growing margins after a few years.

Check all these parameters of the industry and then select some good companies for long-term investment. The more clarity there is in liquidity and solvency, the more consistent will be the profitability. If you have any doubts limit your exposure. The more confident you become, you can increase the weightage of the company.

The decision to pick a stock for the long-term portfolio should come from a good understanding of its growth, consistency and quality. Just growth is not enough without quality. Just quality too is insufficient by itself, as it will be of no use if the company cannot grow its business. We must check these factors in conjunction with each other and make an informed decision. Only those companies with consistent growth and quality will give lifelong income, appreciation and dividends too.

Blindly running after cheap valuations will not get the desired results when it comes to creating a long-term portfolio. Don't decide the list of companies in your portfolio based on cheap **PE (price to earnings)** valuations. Companies with good growth, consistent profits and cash flow generally command higher valuations. So, if you go after the cheapest, you miss out on the best companies. There is no shortcut to a detailed study, and it is good idea to consider all the above-mentioned points before including any stock in your wealth portfolio.

This takes us to the final step: The risk-free and stress-free journey of creating your wealth portfolio, which can grow, stay and pay you for long.

STEP 5

Create the Wealth Portfolio of Assets which Can Stay, Grow and Pay you for Long and Enjoy a Risk-Free and Stress-Free Investment Journey

> The worth of a business is measured not by what has been put into it, but by what can be taken out of it
>
> **– Warren Buffet**

Here we are! We have finally arrived at the most important and practical step, that of portfolio creation.

Tell me, do you wish to create your portfolio of assets independently? Frankly speaking, depending on someone else's tips and assurances will not give you the confidence. By now, you should understand why it's important for you to know the reasons for investing in the stock market. You should be able to select the industries which can grow and within these growth industries, select the strong businesses with good leadership to invest your hard-earned money in. However, risk is a given as far as the stock markets are concerned and so the chief purpose of this chapter is to learn how to reduce your risk, stay focused on your investment strategy and reap better value from your investments.

The question is, do you have the conviction that a company and its businesses are going to grow and generate wealth for the years to come, so that you too can earn year on year and leave a legacy for future generations? Or would you rather lay your trust on the views of other people, including TV commentators, news anchors or some family member's casual discussion? Isn't it better to learn and understand how to build your trust on those few solid businesses which can create a strong foundation for your wealth generating portfolio? It is important that you have your own clarity in the business and how it is running. You must rest assured that you have put your money only in growing economies, growing industries, and top-class companies that can earn wealth now and forever. Thus, you can embark on a stress-free and tension-free journey towards wealth. You should ask yourself this question: *Is the risk I'm taking worth it?* Get ready to start creating your wealth portfolio with value buying. This is Step 5.

At this point, let's quickly recap our journey thus far. As we took the first step, we looked at our personal finances and made that important decision to start planning our investments. We learned how to check and improve our debt situation. We began the journey towards wealth with the repair, reform and transform plan. We worked out a plan to save consistently with discipline and awareness. Hope you are with me on this?

Secondly, we looked at the vitals of world economies through GDP and identified the outperforming economy in which we can expect our savings to grow. We understood the connection between markets and the economy by studying the behaviour of GDP with marketcap.

Next, we learned to categorize the numerous industrial sectors. The main purpose of studying the growing sectors was to understand that it is these sector that create the opportunities for companies to become big. Regardless of how big a company is, if the sector in which it is working is no good, then it will not be able to perform well.

We identified the growing sectors which are the engines of demand, that have been able to generate consistent and significant growth in the economy. We put in the effort to observe the life cycles of these industries. We identified whether they were in the emerging phase, growth phase, maturity phase or decaying phase.

Subsequently, our biggest challenge was to select the top-quality companies from the demanding sectors. We checked the quantitative and qualitative factors that can make small companies grow big and big companies become giants. We saw how there is a tremendous growth potential for our investments in India. Now we are loaded with enough conviction to start investing. Right? We are ready to take the next important step, that of creating a wealth portfolio through a growth strategy, quality strategy and **value buying.** Let us explore this.

Over the past 20 years, Nifty has travelled from 1,000 to 18,000 points. Did it travel in one straight line or were there ups and downs in the journey?

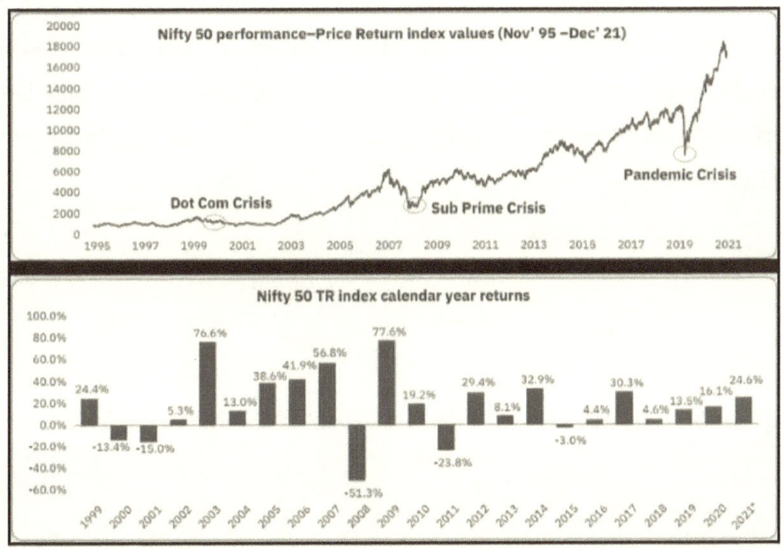

The big falls in the market on several occasions are clearly visible. The reasons behind the fall may be different each time but what happens after the fall? We see a good recovery and later, a rally. Why?

If we invest in an economy that's growing, we may face some hurdles, but a growing economy is always going to boost the sales of its companies and profits are bound to grow. This pushes your valuation up. Right?

We saw the dot com crisis, where we witnessed the fall for two consecutive years with a 13% and 15% damage, respectively. The damage was cleared with a fresh rally after two years. The bigger fall was seen in 2008, where we witnessed the sub-prime crisis, and the global economy was affected. The Indian market witnessed a 51% fall, but it recovered in subsequent years. It fell from 6,300 to 2,300. We saw the pandemic crisis in 2020 and the market crashed, falling from 12,000 to 8,000. Later, it made a quick recovery. Each fall was due to a temporary problem in the economy. Once the economy starts to recover, so does the market.

A similar reaction and reflection of the economy on the stock market is seen in the long-term world index. In the chart below we can see how the market reacted during different situations. Despite the different hurdles that hammered the market, in the long run, the market boomed.

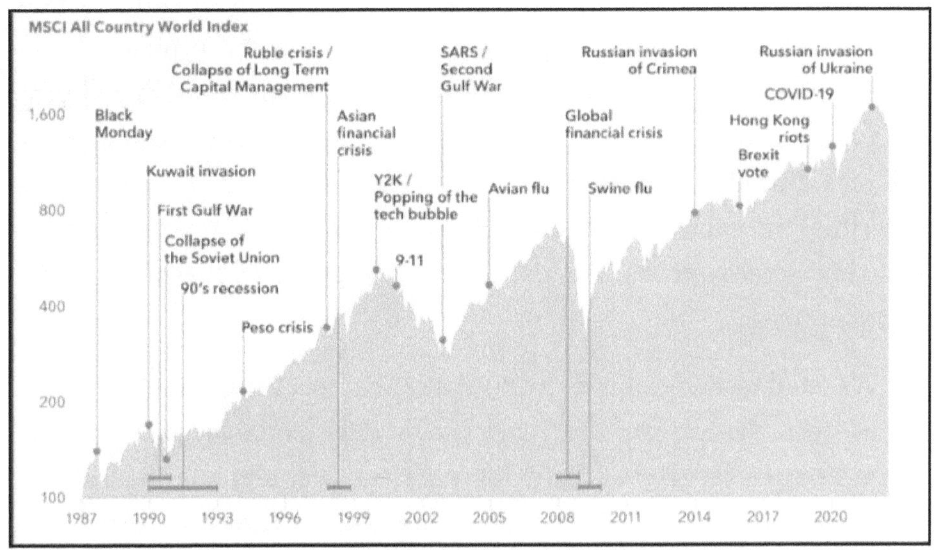

Any market we consider, whether it be S&P_500 or Nifty, the probability of making losses is higher when we invest in the short term. There is a more than 50% probability of making losses if we invest with a one-year time frame. The probability of losses is minimized as we move from the short term to the long term. We can see in the chart how the probability of making losses is nil as per historical data. So, the rule is simple when it comes to investing. 'Time' is the secret word. Investors need patience for wealth creation. The stock market is not an overnight get rich scheme. Patience is the key to success. I repeat, consistency is the mother of mastery. Investors with patience are going to outperform smart investors over the long run. As the great Warren Buffet says: *You cannot have a baby in one month by impregnating nine women.* For anything great to happen, we need time. The Taj Mahal, the Great Wall of China and the Statue of Liberty were not built overnight.

In the initial years, when I was a new investor, my biggest joy was to save myself from big falls like what happened in 2004. I escaped, and was very thrilled about it, but then came 2008 and I was badly hit. Later, I understood that there is no escape from such major falls in market movement. Thus, I decided to tackle the problem head-on, figuring out what should be done during such massive sell offs. Market falls are as inevitable as rallies. We can't escape these massive sell offs. But at the same time, some of our shares are going to grow ten times in value from here. Shocked? The market gives us such amazing opportunities. We just need to make use of these wonderful opportunities.

We need to understand the market and expect reasonable returns. People get demotivated as they have unreasonable expectations. Always be conservative with your expectations, and the market will give you more than you expected. More pain in the short term than what you had expected means more gain in the long term, more than you could have ever imagined.

What is value buying? Value buying is a continuous process. Whenever markets fall due to any reason, even the best companies fall to some extent. The market will give us several such opportunities.

Value buying, also known as value investing, is a stock market investment strategy where investors seek out stocks from growing industries and top-quality companies that are considered undervalued. The idea is to find stocks trading at a price lower than their intrinsic value, based on fundamental analysis of the company's financials, earnings, and other relevant factors.

This does not mean that we should buy all that is available at low prices. Remember what you have learned. Value buying should not come before the growth and quality strategy. Value buying should be undertaken only after the growth and quality analysis. During my 15 years of experience with thousands of investors, I have seen many people misunderstand value buying. They just choose the stock that is trading at low PE, buy it and wait forever. That stock is not going to move. Yet it may give 100% recovery. But we are not here for a 100% normal upside. We are here for a multi-year rally and to get a multi-year rally your company must grow their sales and profits year on year. If your company doesn't grow financially, then the stock price of that company is going to stay at a fair valuation, and it is not going to yield a better return. Just like a quality company alone does not guarantee good returns, value buying alone will not guarantee great returns. Growth is the essential quality in any long-term wealth creator company.

I agree that value investors believe that the market sometimes misprices stocks, creating opportunities for long-term gains when the market corrects itself. They look for stocks that are temporarily out of favour or have been overlooked by other investors, presenting a buying opportunity at low prices. But are these companies from growing industries and are they quality companies? This is an important question to ask yourself before you dive in.

Let us look at some examples:

SAIL, ONGC, IOC, MTNL, HUL, Tata Steel, and SBI were among the largest companies of India before the 21st century began. Most of the companies from the above list were public sector units as pre-liberalization, most businesses were in the hands of PSUs and there were fewer opportunities for private players.

Today, after 20 years of privatization, we see that among the above-mentioned top companies, SAIL is at 157, ONGC is at 28, MTNL is at 700, while SBI has remained at 8. All these companies are also available below the PE (price to earnings ratio) of 15. When we buy the stocks of these companies, apart from SBI, we can't say that we are value buying. Value buying alone does nothing. Except for SBI, the return on our investment was not even on a par with fixed securities. Why? Because their profits did not grow. When I was working in a chemical company, I asked people for some good tips. Guess what tips I got? *"Beta blue chip buy karo."* SAIL, MTNL, IOC, ONGC were all blue chips then. Yes, SBI is a performer in the PSU segment. Why? Because SBI changed with time. They came out with innovative ideas to drive their growth with life insurance, general insurance, AMCs, credit cards and many other businesses. Yet, HDFC Bank, which was nowhere in the early 21st century, is the third in marketcap and profits today. Why? Because HDFC Bank grew while those in the list above did not. So, what worked? Growth worked better than value. As an investor, you need to identify quality companies from growing industries and then look out for value buying opportunities in the falling market. I hope you got the message.

Here are a few real-life examples of companies that have been considered value stocks in the past. Please note that these examples are based on historical data and may not reflect the current market conditions.

Coca-Cola: The leading beverages player was in correction between 1987 and 1990. Yes, the industry was the fastest growing, but due to a challenging near-term environment, we saw the correction. A similar correction was seen between 1991 and 1994. We saw a strong correction from 1998 to 2015. Despite everything, Coca-Cola, which was trading at around USD 0.7 in 1980, is close to USD 61 today. This is more than a 100X return, but what is more important is that a quality company from a growing industry yields regular dividends that can grow over a period. Even during bad times of correction, investors will receive consistent dividends. So why worry? If you have invested, you are going to get consistent dividends lifelong as long as the world drinks Coke. Investors who saw potential in the company's turnaround efforts and long-term growth prospects were able to cash in on the growth story.

There are several stories of such companies. You will have to search for these stories to be convinced about your long-term wealth investment.

State Bank of India (SBI): SBI has been considered a value stock by some investors due to its low valuation metrics, such as price-to-earnings (P/E) ratio and price-to-book (P/B) ratio. Investors have recognized SBI as the largest public sector bank in India with a strong market position and potential for future growth. The stock was available at cheap valuations for a long time, from 2010 to 2020.

TCS: The leading IT software company has also provided similar opportunities. We saw the great fall from Rs 300 to Rs 100 in 2008. We saw the correction in 2011 from Rs 600 to Rs 450. What were we supposed to do? Value buy growth stocks. We saw the fall from Rs 1,400 to Rs 1,000 in 2015. The movement of any stock is not in our control. What is in our control? Value buying and increasing the stakes in companies where we have great conviction. We saw the correction in 2018 from Rs 2,200 to Rs 1,600 – another great opportunity for value buying. Despite all these corrections, we saw consistent and growing dividend yields.

Successful investors grab such opportunities when the market is down, investing in top-quality companies. Only during a fall, do the prices come down. Even the best companies are available at reasonable valuations during such times. The motto is, 'Buy during a fall and avoid buying during a rally.' It's as simple as that.

My investing experience has proved to me time and again that 50% correction is normal in several stocks. This does not mean that the company is bad. These are just reflections of short-term challenges in the market and fear among investors. Several stocks from my holdings have corrected 50% or more but post the correction phase there was a multi-year rally. Britannia, for example, came down to 125 from

250. I took this opportunity to value buy. Again, if what we bought at 2,000 comes down to 1,000, it's a chance to value buy. There's no need to worry. Today, most of those shares have grown 20 times from the initial purchase price.

Every stock falls and appreciates. During the fall, it corrects because the industry may be under pressure or there could be inflationary pressures, etc. There may be several different reasons, but ask yourself the following questions during such times: *Is the company going to close? Is it going to perform very badly due to this situation or is it just a temporary set-back?* If the answer is 'No,' then just buy. Because over time, your company will give you a very good return on your investment. Continue your SIP (systematic investment plan) during every fall. People who don't track the fundamental data and results run after companies when there is positive news everywhere and the market is rallying because they have this fear of losing out. Those who are looking for excitement become happy only during rallies and fear investing in good companies during market corrections. Such people do not earn well. To earn long-term wealth, we need to undertake value buying in growth sectors.

Only under one condition will people not be able to earn from markets, and that is, if they get frightened and sell their holdings during any fall or if they sell off their well-selected stocks for a small 15–20% profit. What is the biggest hurdle to building a wealth portfolio? Yes, *'Gabbar Khud,'* because the market does perform in the long run. But if our mindset is hyperactive, we may disturb the growth potential of our investments.

Why do markets fall?

We have travelled from a 0.5 trillion to 3 trillion marketcap, but this has not come in one straight line. Problems are bound to come on the way. It is quite natural. Corrections do happen in even the best stocks and can last for long periods as it happened in the case of TCS. I have seen my companies fall with a correction of more than 50%. But having conviction in the improving fundamentals of India and some patience have always paid off.

Demand may get affected in the short term; you may witness your estimates and projections of company sales and profits take a deep dive. Their businesses may be muted for some time, as was the case with Wonderla in the amusement parks space, when the world came to a standstill due to Covid-19. But when the scenario changed, people came out in hordes and the demand for these outdoor-activity-oriented companies was back with a bang. Their profits also improved.

Occasionally, inflation hits the economy, and the prices of products begin to rise. Commodity and raw material prices rise and pinch the pockets of manufacturing companies, impacting their profit margins. Big corporations with popular brands, who can increase their selling prices, survive such bouts of inflation, but smaller companies bear the brunt, and their profit margins are badly affected. We saw this recently when the price of crude oil was hyped as a result of the US sanctions against Russian crude oil. Most manufacturing companies in the secondary sector saw a huge jump in raw-material prices and their operating expenses increased. Strong companies like Asian Paints, who have better pricing power in their hands, managed to step up their prices and hold their margins above other competitors, while smaller players got pushed behind. As a cascading effect, their stock prices also fell hard. Wars, inflation, political instability, economic upheavals, natural calamities, pandemics like Covid-19, etc., any of these unpredictable occurrences may lead to a market fall. A long-term investor is bound to see such events during the investment period. So be prepared for many more villains. But the rule should be: Buy during a fall and avoid buying during rallies.

I never tire from repeating this rule. Way back in the 1950s, Mr. Benjamin Graham wrote these words in his widely acclaimed book *The Intelligent Investor* on value investing, and the rule holds true even to this day.

We must try to understand what actually happens with the increase and decrease in stock prices. How does it create a better opportunity or value for us?

Let me give you another example. Let's say, your EPS (earnings per share) of a company is Rs. 100 and it distributes around 50% dividends every year. So, your dividend is Rs. 50. The price of the company is going to travel up and down due to near-term challenges. If the price of the company rallies to Rs 2,000 we can say the company is trading at 2,000/100, a PE of 20. The yield is 100/2,000 = 5% and the dividend yield is 2.5%. When the same company falls and is available at Rs 1,000, then the company is trading at 1,000/100, a PE of 10. The yield for the same company is 100/1,000 = 10% while dividend yield is 50/1,000 = 5%. Tell me, should you buy the stock at Rs 2,000 or at Rs 1,000? Is the company any different when trading at Rs 2,000 and Rs 1,000? No. The company is the same, but the challenges and insights are different. Where should you buy for a high yield? At a low price. But guess where people tend to buy the stocks? At the Rs 2,000 price! Why? Because the atmosphere is positive at Rs 2,000, while the atmosphere is negative at Rs 1,000 and investors are highly influenced by the way things seem to look rather than the actual reality. To become a successful investor, you need to get out of this mindset.

To be fearful when others are greedy, and greedy when others are fearful

– Warren Buffet

Value buying is a continuous process: Please find below the Nifty chart.

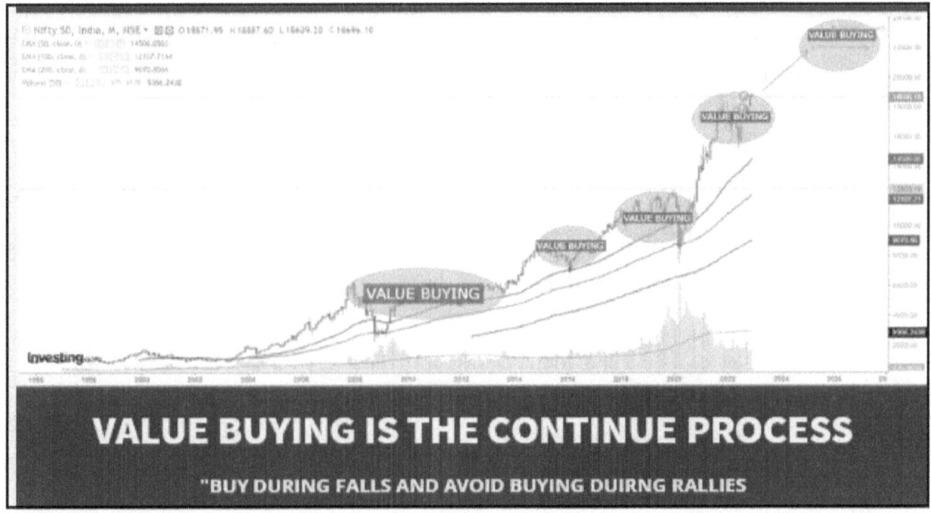

Talking of valuations, there are several fundamental indicators that tell us if a company's stock price is expensive or cheap. The **PE** or price to earnings ratio is a very popular ratio. Fast-growing companies generally command higher price to earnings because market players are willing to pay a higher price in anticipation of higher future growth in these businesses.

Understand that PE = growth.

PE is directly related to the company's profit growth. The more the growth, the higher the PE.

Therefore, you may find that high growth companies will always be more expensive, whereas companies in the same sector with a lower growth rate continue to remain at a low PE. Investors who are on the lookout for only PE ratios to decide if a company is good for their portfolio or not commit the blunder of running after low PE stocks and clutter their portfolios with unwanted scrips.

During market corrections, even high growth/high PE companies are available at cheaper prices. Their PE ratios fall, but this is not the time to panic. This is the time to go ahead and accumulate those selected high growth stocks. If you combine PE and growth, you get the term PEG. What is the PEG ratio?

The PEG ratio, also known as the price/earnings growth ratio, is a financial metric used by investors to assess the valuation of a stock relative to its expected earnings growth. It is calculated by dividing the price-to-earnings (P/E) ratio of a stock by its projected earnings growth rate.

The formula for calculating the PEG ratio is as follows:

PEG Ratio = P/E Ratio / Annual Earnings Growth Rate

The PEG ratio is useful in value buying as it helps investors determine whether a stock is overvalued or undervalued, considering its growth prospects. Here's how the PEG ratio is interpreted:

PEG ratio less than 1: It is generally considered as an indication that the stock may be undervalued. It suggests that the stock's price is relatively low compared to its expected earnings growth, making it potentially attractive for value investors.

PEG ratio around 1: It indicates that the stock's valuation is in line with its expected earnings growth rate. It suggests that the stock is accurately valued and may not be significantly overvalued or undervalued.

PEG ratio greater than 1: It may indicate that the stock is overvalued relative to its earnings growth rate. It suggests that the stock's price is relatively high compared to its expected growth, which could potentially make it less attractive for value investors.

While the PEG ratio can be a useful tool in value investing, it is important to note its limitations. The PEG ratio relies on the projected earnings growth, which can be uncertain and subject to change. Additionally, the PEG ratio does not account for other factors such as industry dynamics, competitive position and overall market conditions, which should also be considered when making investment decisions.

Value investors often use multiple valuation metrics and conduct comprehensive fundamental analysis to assess the attractiveness of a stock. The PEG ratio can be a valuable addition to this analysis, providing insights into the relationship between a stock's price, earnings and the expected growth.

Buying when the expected yield is better is also a good value buying strategy. When is your stock's yield expected to be better? When the earnings are going to increase or if the stock has fallen due to market conditions despite improved earnings.

Buying at lower valuations improves your **yield**. What does it mean? It means that you pay less (in terms of price) to earn more (by way of dividends and price appreciation). If you become smart and buy during a fall, you earn a better yield. But if you wake up too late and buy only once the stock price has shot up, then your yield goes down overall.

The concept of yield is quite simple. If you invest Rs. 100 in a FD at an interest of 6%, it means that your yield is Rs. 6. In stocks, your earnings come from the dividends the company distributes to its shareholders. Whether you buy your stock at Rs. 100 or Rs. 200, you are going to earn only a fixed amount as dividend per share. To improve your yield, would it not be smarter for you to take the opportunity and buy the share whenever it is available at a lower price range? In this way, you can even double your yield and improve your returns to a great extent.

Expect your yield to cross the benchmark of fixed securities initially and aim to accelerate and overtake all other investments in the long run.

You can also expect the **book value** of your selected companies to rise year on year. Most companies which are cash rich, and the cash flow is consistent, will show a healthy increase in their book value. Check it regularly as it indicates the actual incremental value of your share in the books of the company. If the book value is rising, then you can expect the price of the stock also to appreciate well in the markets.

Creating an equity wealth portfolio involves a systematic approach to selecting and managing a diversified range of equity investments. I was doing exactly the opposite of this initially. Let me show you some steps that can help you create an equity wealth portfolio:

Step 1: Define Your Goals and Risk Tolerance

Start by determining your investment goals and understanding your risk tolerance. Are you looking for long-term growth, income or a combination of both? Consider your financial objectives, time horizon and how comfortable you are with market fluctuations. To do this you need to first identify your financial goals. These can include short-term goals (e.g., saving for a vacation or down payment on a house), medium-term goals (e.g., paying for education or buying a car) and long-term goals (e.g., retirement planning or building wealth for the future).

Example: Let's say your financial goal is to save for retirement. You have 25 years until retirement age and want to accumulate substantial wealth to facilitate a comfortable lifestyle during your retirement years. Hence, you should understand the importance of all the different asset classes. Fixed securities are also important along with growth investments like equity.

Step 2: Research and Education

Try to develop a solid understanding of equity investments. Educate yourself on the various investment strategies, types of asset classes, sectors and market trends. Use reputable financial news sources, investment books and online resources to enhance your knowledge. Annual reports of the company you track are highly useful to understand their businesses. Attending their conference calls is also highly useful to get near-term insights.

Step 3: Asset Allocation

Determine the appropriate asset allocation based on your goals and risk tolerance. Asset allocation refers to the distribution of your investment across different asset classes, such as equities, bonds and cash. Decide what percentage of your portfolio will be allocated to equities and FS. We have already discussed this earlier. Do understand that both are useful.

Step 4: Diversification

Diversification is crucial to reducing risk. Allocate your equity investments across different sectors, industries, geographies, business groups and company sizes. This spreads your risk and helps protect your portfolio from being overly exposed to a single investment or sector.

Step 5: Stock Selection

If you decide to invest in individual stocks, conduct thorough research on the companies you are considering. Analyze their financial statements, earnings growth, competitive advantages and management teams. Consider using fundamental analysis techniques to evaluate potential investments.

Step 6: Review and Re-adjust Your Portfolio Regularly

Periodically review your portfolio to ensure it aligns with your goals and risk tolerance. Rebalance your portfolio, if necessary, by increasing or decreasing your weightage in sectors to maintain your desired asset allocation. For example, if you have invested in the banking sector and you see that the credit growth is not so strong or the GNPA% is increasing, this means that this sector will probably face a challenging time. Considering this, you can decrease the weightage in this sector till the situation returns to normal. Increase the weightage when you see the fundamentals improving. Everything is temporary in the market. Both bad and good times are only temporary, as markets move in cycles. You should increase or decrease and re-adjust your holdings in the asset classes as necessary. For example, if you see that the growth is softening, inflation is increasing or some challenging economic indicators are present, you should increase the weightage in fixed securities like FDs or gold as the situation may last for a long period. Similarly, if you see things improving, you should grab the opportunity to increase the weightage in equity at lucrative prices before the market again shoots up. Regularly monitor the performance of your holdings and make adjustments as needed.

Step 7: Risk Management

Implement risk management strategies to protect your portfolio. If you see that the sector you invested in is going through a challenging time and long-term growth is not visible, you should exit from this sector and divert the money to growth sectors to optimize your portfolio. For example, the print media business is suffering due to digital media. Investing in print media can generate lower yield than expected as growth is not aggressive. What should you do? Divert the money. Similarly, when some company is caught in bad corporate governance, be alert. Lord Krishna said: If you are cheated, it is not your fault, but if you are cheated twice, it is your fault. Once you get the hint of bad governance, stay away from such companies. It is always better to invest in good companies at higher prices than to invest in bad companies at cheap prices.

Step 8: Monitor and Stay Informed

Stay informed about market trends, economic developments and any news that may impact your investments. Stay disciplined and avoid making impulsive decisions based on short-term market fluctuations. I avoid watching TV all the time, but I'm aware of the happenings in the companies I've invested in through the Corporate Announcements section available on the BSEIndia website.

Remember, creating an equity wealth portfolio requires time, research and continuous monitoring. It's essential to stay patient and focused on your long-term goals while adjusting your portfolio as needed.

You need a proper investment strategy for all this to work out without any confusion, doubt, fear, greed or emotions interfering and distracting you from your main purpose.

Since I did not follow a disciplined approach in the initial years of my investment journey, I wasted a lot of time, energy and money. I learned the hard way by making mistakes. So let me share some of my learnings with you.

The rules to follow for a good investment strategy are:

1. **Do not speculate**: Speculation is a sponsored industry. People may brag and boast about their bumper earnings, but no one speaks about their losses. Futures and options, leverage, etc., are sponsored programmes. Speculation is dangerous; you may recall how King Yudhishtir in the Mahabharat lost

everything due to speculation and gambling. Wealth is not created through speculation.

Do you think big businesses have grown due to speculation? The largest companies and corporations are built for long-term growth on strong fundamentals and ethical management practices, not on speculation.

2. **Do not leverage**: Stock markets become very attractive at highs and many people get tempted to pump in funds at any cost at such times. People would call me and ask if they could take loans to invest in the markets. Please do not take such rash and fancy actions. What if the market goes down? No one can guarantee good, consistent returns. You must pay the interest on your loans regardless of whether the market moves up or down. Overconfidence about market returns is never a good idea. Invest less, but it should be your money. You don't need too much money to create wealth. I have seen people with lots of money end up with no money. I have also seen investors who have created huge wealth with very little money. It is not how much you invest; it's all about how you invest.

3. **Have a balanced investment, 50/50**: Equity can be volatile in the short term. Never put all your money in the market. Keep at least 50% of your savings in fixed securities. Fixed securities give a good buffer during difficult times. Equities earn good returns, but it comes with volatility in the short term, whereas fixed securities earn less but are more stable. Both are required for a balanced investment portfolio. Some people avoid fixed securities and lean too much towards markets and others think markets are not for them. These are extreme approaches. What we need is a 50/50 investment approach which can tide over good and bad times.

4. **Diversify in different industry sectors**: Diversification is the best solution to achieve both safety and growth. As retail investors we need to be protected from high risk. Some people go crazy after certain industries, making huge investments, concentrating all their funds in few industries. This method may work for big mutual funds but for small investors it can be risky. Particular industries may grow big, while some may go out of business in the long run, leaving us with nothing to show even after many years of toil. So let us not put all our eggs in one basket. Do not put more than 15% of your money in any single industry.

5. **Diversify in different companies.** Select the best companies from a wide variety of sectors and adjust your weightage in these companies. At certain times, pharma companies perform well, as was the case during Covid-19, but soon, the craze for pharma stocks died down. There was also a rush to buy US-based IT companies but inflation and disruptions in the US markets made it lukewarm. Concentrating just on one particular country, industry or company is not a good idea. The idea is to reduce risk and not be too invested in one company or market. Diversification is the best medicine for risk in the market. Do not put more than 7% of your money in a single company.

6. **Stocks will fall 50% and rally 100%. Both are normal**: But this will seem normal only to those who have diversified their portfolios. All others with concentrated investments are bound to be disappointed and disheartened during such volatility.

7. **Buy during falls**: Accumulate the stocks from your list during market dips. Those who buy during falls enjoy the rallies and they need not worry about the high buying prices during rallies.

8. **Consistency in the first three years is the toughest**: You may see your portfolio moving up by 50% in one year and the very next year itself it may fall by 35% or more. This kind of roller-coaster movement is normal but tough to digest for newcomers. A person who can keep his investment routine consistent and mind fixed on the long-term vision can achieve his objective. Approximately, the first three years is the most testing time to get accustomed to the constant movement in prices. You must not be too happy or too depressed due to price volatility. Just give it time. You have already done the research and selected the gems of the economy, so you are bound to reap good returns. Don't get too worried about price changes. Keep yourself abreast of the changes in the business and their quarterly and annual results. This is the one thing that gave me constant reassurance and kept me on track with firm focus on my purpose.

Let us examine the meaning of risk. What do we mean by risk? Risk, in simple terms, means that due to some unforeseen reasons, you may not get an expected return from your investment. One thing is clear; there is always risk embedded in most investments. No one can run away from it. Instead, you must try to understand the risk and find ways to reduce it to some extent. In our previous discussion, we understood that diversification is one of the ways to reduce risk. Let us check the kind of risks we may have to handle.

We may categorize risk under two basic heads. Systematic risk and unsystematic risk. Both are going to appear at some point or the other.

Systematic risk comprises those difficult situations that affect the whole economy. This is also known as market risk. Market risk refers to the overall risk inherent in the broader financial market. It is influenced by macroeconomic factors, geopolitical events, interest rates and market sentiment. Market risk affects the entire equity market and can cause fluctuations in stock prices. Even well-diversified portfolios are subject to market risk, which cannot be eliminated fully through diversification. We saw how the **inflation** which shot up due to war had a spill over effect on crude oil prices, food prices, trade disruptions, etc. Due to inflations, the central bank hiked the interest rates around the world. This led to an increase in the borrowing cost of companies. Thus, interest rates align with commodity prices, increasing the total cost of production. Consequently, the prices of all goods and services were inflated. Companies' profit margins dropped drastically even though they witnessed sales growth, as we saw in FY2023. We saw inflationary price rise in many discretionary items, electronic goods, food products, etc., which took a direct hit. Inflation is a risk all economies face. It puts temporary pressure on the economy, which may last a few years. As normalcy returns, we may see an upturn in the performances of companies.

So be prepared for these inevitabilities like high interest rates, recession, natural and unnatural manmade disasters, wars, etc., which are systematic risks the economy is bound to face. As a result of these risks, our investments may get impacted. The way to reduce the risk to some extent is to diversify your funds. Keep some liquidity always for emergencies and avoid pouring all your savings into one basket. Systematic risks can affect the portfolio for a few years. This does not mean that investing in stocks is bad. Markets may remain range bound in correction mode for some time and once the situation eases then markets recover and may even rally. So have patience and do not panic about your long-term holdings.

Just because your shares doubled in one year don't expect it to happen every year. Don't expect a 50% growth rate every year, not even 25%. A reasonable expectation is for markets to give a 15%

CAGR, if you manage your portfolio intelligently without falling prey to emotions. And mind you, a 15% CAGR is a pretty good return in the long term.

Let's move on to unsystematic risk, which involves company-specific risk.

Company-specific risk, also known as unsystematic risk, is specific to individual companies. It arises from factors such as management decisions, competitive position, financial performance, regulatory changes or disruptions in the industry. Company-specific risk can have a significant impact on the value of individual stocks and can be reduced through diversification across different companies and sectors.

Unsystematic risk is associated with poor management of the company, litigations, and regulatory changes which adversely affect a company. They are considered unsystematic because they affect one company more than others. So be prepared. These things are inevitable. This may affect your returns on your company. You must be alert about these things to take the critical decision of whether to remain invested in the company or not.

For example, a decade ago, we saw such a risk in Welspun India when they claimed they offered quality products but did not deliver. We saw the same risk in PC Jeweller a few years ago. Even in the beverage sector, we saw Manpasand doing gimmicks with the GST. We saw some instances in Vakrangee also.

According to new norms by SEBI we saw the changes in Asset Management Companies (AMC) charges, which affected the overall revenue of the entire AMC industry. We saw the correction in AMC companies post this reform. So do not assume that all reform is beneficial to companies. The reforms were beneficial to customers, but it hit the AMC companies hard.

In another instance, we saw the Railways increasing the royalty on ticketing. This could affect the revenue of Indian Railways Catering and Tourism Corporation (IRCTC). Later, they withdrew it, but if it had been implemented, it would have impacted IRCTC revenues. We should be prepared for the possibility of another royalty share hike announcement, but this time, a lower hike.

Over the next 10 to 15 years, your investments are going to be exposed to several systematic and unsystematic risks. This may impact your company's stock price, for a while at least. This is okay, there's no need to worry. You may see low demand risk, inflation risk, geopolitical tensions between countries and political instability. Yes, these affect the market, but in the long term, your companies are going to perform. Understanding these risks is essential for long-term equity portfolio management. Diversification, thorough research, and periodic portfolio reviews can help manage these risks effectively. It's also important to align your investment strategy with your risk tolerance, time horizon and financial goals.

Creating the Wealth Portfolio: The Master Steps

1. Create a proper investment portfolio and follow a disciplined strategy. Do not buy and sell frequently in your long-term investments.

2. Search and invest in growing countries: Growing countries will give a boost to industries, and this will in turn boost the performance of the companies you have invested in.

3. Segregate top quality companies that are sustainable and can give consistent cash flow.

4. Check the historical sales volume growth of the companies you track.

For example, if you plan to invest in a retail finance company like Bajaj Finance, you should know whether their AUM is growing or not, and if it is growing, at what percentage it is growing.

For example, if you plan to invest in a cement company like Ultratech, you should know whether their production is growing or not and if its growing, then at what percentage? How many metric tonnes of cement are they selling year on year and is this figure increasing?

For example, if you plan to invest in a passenger car company like Maruti, you should know if their car sales volumes are growing or not and if its growing, then at what percentage.

For example, if you plan to invest in an amusement park company like Wonderla, you should know whether their footfalls are growing or not and if its growing, then at what percentage.

Similarly, you should track the volumes of different companies. The below chart can be useful.

VOLUME (REAL GROWTH)

ARE THE VOLUME OF YOUR INVESTED COMPANIES GROWING?

BELOW ARE SOME INDICATORS WHICH TRIGGER THE GROWTH.

COMPANIES Year	ULTRATECH VOLUME(MMT)	RELAXO Pairs	JUBLFOOD RESTAURANT	BAJAJ FINANCE AUM	MARUTI Vehicles	WONDERLA VISITORS LAKH	Dr. Lalpathlabs labs	DMART STORE	TEAMLEASE HEADCOUNT	AFFLE USERS in CR
fy_2005	15									
fy_2006	16	5.1								
fy_2007	18	5.2	130							
fy_2008	17	6.4	181	2478						
fy_2009	18	6.8	241	2539						
fy_2010	20	8.4	306	4032	1018365	16				
fy_2011	35	8.7	378	7573	1271005	20				
fy_2012	41	9.3	465	13107	1133695	23	125			
fy_2013	41	10	586	17517	1171434	23	131			
fy_2014	41	10.8	752	24067	1155041	23	146			
fy_2015	45	12.3	930	32410	1292415	23	164			
fy_2016	48	13.6	1097	44229	1429248	23	172			
fy_2017	49	13.5	1117	60196	1568603	27	182	135		
fy_2018	63	15.7	1134	82422	1779574	25	193	155	187270	4
fy_2019	85	18.4	1227	115888	1862449	25	200	176	222158	6
fy_2020	82	17.9	1335	147153	1563297	24	216	214	220210	7
fy_2021	85	19.1	1360	152947	1457861	4	231	236	228150	11
fy_2022	93	17.5	1567	192087	1652653	10	277	284	285230	20
fy_2023	106	17.1	1816	247379	1966164	33	277	324	282450	26

The decrease in volumes may trigger a slow down or cause you to lose out on the competitive edge. Decrease in volume, if seen in the whole industry, must be an industry-related challenge. If it is seen in only a particular company, then it must be a company related challenge. Right?

5. You should check the historical sales growth of the companies you track. It provides insights that the company has potential for better growth than the volumes. Generally, if there's a 5–7% volume growth, then you can expect a 10–12% sales revenue growth, as companies with strong brand value and pricing power can even increase their prices.

COMPANIES Year	ULTRATECH REVENUE	RELAXO REVENU	JUBLFOOD REVENUE	BAJAJ FINANCE REVENUE	MARUTI REVENUE	WONDERLA REVENUE	Dr. Lalpathlabs REVENUE	DMART REVENUE	TEAMLEASE REVENUE	AFFLE REVENUE
fy_2005	2703	216	74	173	13343					
fy_2006	3261	201	97	243	12481					
fy_2007	4972	236	139	402	15252					
fy_2008	5609	306	211	503	18824	30				
fy_2009	6487	408	281	599	21454	63				
fy_2010	7172	554	424	916	29623	70				
fy_2011	13497	686	678	1406	37040	91			698	
fy_2012	18313	860	1018	2172	35587	115	320	2209	934	
fy_2013	20175	1005	1408	3110	43588	139	424	3341	1262	
fy_2014	20280	1206	1724	4173	44524	156	544	4687	1538	
fy_2015	22936	1481	2082	5418	50802	192	640	6439	2019	
fy_2016	25552	1712	2416	7333	58208	223	786	8588	2505	72
fy_2017	29294	1652	2561	9989	79546	278	908	11881	3064	66
fy_2018	32888	1949	3003	12757	84040	278	1056	15009	3640	167
fy_2019	37379	2292	3578	18500	88630	292	1203	20005	4448	249
fy_2020	42125	2411	3997	26386	75611	283	1330	24870	5201	334
fy_2021	44726	2359	3312	26683	70333	45	1581	24143	4882	517
fy_2022	52589	2654	4396	31641	88296	128	2087	30976	6480	1082
fy_2023	63239	2783	5158	41397	117571	429	2017	42839	7870	1434

The past does not guarantee future growth, but it gives us an indication of possible future growth, provided we track the industry and their volumes. We can track long-term growth and short-term growth along with some industry inputs to estimate future growth.

6. Check the historical profit growth of the companies in the same way you track volume and sales. It will give you a clear picture of whether your company will generate positive cash flow during vulnerable times, or whether it will run into losses. Be prepared that your company is going to face challenging times in the next 10 to 15 years. During the challenging times,

if your company starts making losses, then it is not the right company to invest in. Below is one example of the leading passenger car company, Maruti. The chart shows that despite the challenging time for the automobile industry between FY2019 and FY2022, when volumes were low and sales were affected, Maruti continuously generated cash flow, both for investors and the company. You can trust such companies to generate positive cash flow in the future.

Year	Vehicles	Sales	Profit	MARGIN %
FY_2004		9751	542	6%
FY_2005		13343	854	6%
FY_2006		12481	1189	10%
FY_2007		15252	1562	10%
FY_2008		18824	1731	9%
FY_2009		21454	1219	6%
FY_2010	1018365	29623	2498	8%
FY_2011	1271005	37040	2289	6%
FY_2012	1133695	35587	1635	5%
FY_2013	1171434	43588	2392	5%
FY_2014	1155041	44524	2783	6%
FY_2015	1292415	50802	3711	7%
FY_2016	1429248	58208	4571	8%
FY_2017	1568603	79546	7338	9%
FY_2018	1779574	84040	7722	9%
FY_2019	1862449	88630	7651	9%
FY_2020	1563297	75611	5651	7%
FY_2021	1457861	70333	4230	6%
FY_2022	1652653	88296	3766	4%
FY_2023	1966164	117571	8211	7%

7. You should check the historical price behaviour of your company during good times and bad times. This will help you know the historical fair PE of the company. In this way, you will get guidance regarding future price behaviour. Such

an analysis will clearly tell you when the company is near its fair valuation, where you have a high margin of safety and low risk. Ascertaining the fair valuation helps you avoid investing in companies where the risk is high, and the margin of safety is low. For more than a decade, we have been successfully using this indicator. It has tremendously optimized our fund performance. This is the real optimiser for your fund performance too. Let me show you an example.

Year	Vehicles	Sales	Profit	MARGIN %	High Price	Low Price	HIGHPE	LOWPE
FY_2004		9751	542	6%	588	155	31.3	8.3
FY_2005		13343	854	6%	600	300	20.3	10.2
FY_2006		12481	1189	10%	943	393	22.4	9.3
FY_2007		15252	1562	10%	975	655	16.3	10.9
FY_2008		18824	1731	9%	1248	700	23.1	12.9
FY_2009		21454	1219	6%	855	433	20.8	10.5
FY_2010	1018365	29623	2498	8%	1737	741	20.1	8.6
FY_2011	1271005	37040	2289	6%	1585	1122	20	14.2
FY_2012	1133695	35587	1635	5%	1429	900	25.2	15.9
FY_2013	1171434	43588	2392	5%	1634	1051	20.6	13.3
FY_2014	1155041	44524	2783	6%	1980	1215	21.5	13.2
FY_2015	1292415	50802	3711	7%	3790	1872	30.9	15.2
FY_2016	1429248	58208	4571	8%	4790	3200	31.7	21.1
FY_2017	1568603	79546	7338	9%	6234	3418	25.7	14.1
FY_2018	1779574	84040	7722	9%	9996	6021	39	23.5
FY_2019	1862449	88630	7651	9%	9929	6318	39.2	24.9
FY_2020	1563297	75611	5651	7%	7759	4037	41.5	21.6
FY_2021	1457861	70333	4230	6%	8329	4001	59.5	28.6
FY_2022	1652653	88296	3766	4%	9050	6400	72.6	51.3
FY_2023	1966164	117571	8211	7%	9769	7062	35.9	26

A study of the historical data clearly indicates the fair valuations. Get into the habit of buying at a low PE and avoid buying at a high PE.

8. Check the current trend of volumes, sales, margins and profits as these indicate the near-term range. If volume and sales are growing, it indicates that there is no problem in the demand. If margins are stable, it indicates that sales will be converted to profits. The opposite is also true. If sales and volume are suffering, it's time to be cautious. Similarly, if margins are decreasing, it's time to be cautious.

9. You should stay invested for the long term and reap the fruits. The seed you have planted will be converted to a giant tree

over time and will bear fruits for a lifetime. Investing once and receiving incremental cash flow for lifelong is real wealth. Right?

I hope the above nine steps will provide you a guideline for value buying on your journey towards wealth. This is what big fish do. They invest, expect the company to grow big and reap the fruits.

Do remember the following while creating your assets:

- Six per cent is the base return you get in any FD; all other returns should be above that.
- Assets should be well-balanced with risks and rewards (rule of 50/50).
- Assets should provide a lifelong passive income.
- Assets should take care of all costs.

Let me summarize the key takeaways, with a sense of reflection and inspiration.

Do remember, you are investing in a business; hence, understand the businesses. You are investing for long term wealth; do not have the speculative short-term profits mindset. The stock market can help you create wealth over a period, even exceeding your expectations. At the same time, it can also destroy your happiness and wealth if you fall prey to speculations.

Do remember how to identify growing countries, how to search for growing industries, how to search for companies with long term growth potential, and how to value buy during your journey, whenever you get the opportunity. Yes, it is true that no opportunity is the last opportunity, but it is also true that no two opportunities are similar.

Do remember all the inspiring investment success stories. The more people I meet and hear their success stories, the more confident

I become. I have met various people across the country, some with a good education, while others are college dropouts like me, yet they are successful. I have met both scientists and farmers who have invested and are moving further in life gracefully. I have met professionals and housewives breaking all barriers and creating lifelong assets for their family. I have met young students and even retired people, both growing their wealth risk free and stress free. Hence, I conclude that age, background, sex, and profession are not hurdles in your wealth story.

Who knows? The next time I could be sharing your success story to inspire other investors. See you at the top!

Conclusion

Notes: Recap the chapters. Revise personal finance and how to invest your savings in a proper wealth portfolio spreading it across different asset classes. Define long-term investing, long-term mindset versus momentum trading, your purpose, objectives and goals, and how to execute your plan. Beat the benchmarks. Revise, refresh, repeat.

How to create your stock market portfolio: Stock selection, diversification, weightage. Dividend and yield. Tracking results, systematic investment and fund management. Buy during falls and avoid buying during rallies.

Market cycles – The 10-year time period and how to manage it. How to continue your journey without fear or greed.

Short notes: What to do when your company incurs losses sometimes due to unforeseen circumstances like inflation, etc. (check book value)

Continuous learning; 1% self-improvement plan; upgrade skills.

Model portfolios if required.

The first step is to check and improve your personal finance.

Search out a healthy and growing economy. Know the vitals of your economy.

The third step is to see which sectors are flourishing in that economy.

The fourth step is to sieve out the leaders in those sectors – companies that generate the best sales, have good margins and know how to maintain a healthy balance between debt and equity.

Finally, create a strategy for fabulous and safe returns consistently over the long term. Rebalance your portfolio from time to time by tracking annual and quarterly results.

▪ ▪ ▪

Author's Profile

Piyush Patel is the Founder of PROFITFROMIT, hailed as India's top stock market training institute by Silicon Valley publishers. He has trained several successful research analysts and advisers across India and is the favourite trainer of thousands of small investors too. His talent in explaining tough financial topics in a simple, jargon-free language, and his immense patience to teach, whether the student is a teenager, an analyst or a housewife, with the same amount of interest, is highly laudable. He is highly respected by his students and colleagues for his deep understanding of stock markets, his in-depth inputs and practical approach.

He conducts regular house-full review programmes of a portfolio company's annual and quarterly results analysis, where he provides students with opportunities to present company results, growth analysis and future estimates in a systematic and well-researched manner.

Coming from a simple teacher's family from the city of Baroda, Piyush Patel, who initially started his career in the chemical industry, followed his passion for wealth creation with a strong resolve. In the initial years, he too made mistakes and had to undergo the *'agni pariksha'* of the stock markets. He faced a roller-coaster of profits and losses, but soon enough, he learned not to repeat his mistakes. "It is only perseverance and continuous self-improvement that has made me upgrade myself. I have helped several of my students to turn their portfolio into a golden goose. Upgrading your knowledge and skills sees you through the difficult times."

As a strong believer in nurturing a positive work–life balance, he spends ample time with his family, trekking and travelling regularly with his two intelligent, lovely daughters. Mr. Patel has a black belt in Tae-Kwon-Do, is an avid reader and a popular YouTuber too.

Testimonals

Name: Samir Bipinchandra Shah

City: Mumbai

Profession: Equity Investment Advisor

IT WAS A TOTAL 360 DEGREE CHANGE OF MY MINDSET AFTER ATTENDING THIS WORKSHOP I CHANGED MY MINDSET FROM MAKING SMALL PROFITS IN SHORT TERM TRADES TO MAKING GOOD WEALTH FROM LONG TERM INVESTMENT REALLY THANK YOU FOR ALL PIYUSH SIR AND HIS VERY SUPPORTIVE TEAM.

Name: Vijay Kumar

City: Ludhiana

Profession: Accountant

यह कोर्स मैंने किया और मुझे स्टॉक मार्केट की काफी अच्छी नॉलेज हो गई है और यह कोर्स बहुत ही अच्छे तरीके और आसान तरीके से सिखाता है और यह कोर्स करने के बाद बेल्थ क्रिएट करने के लिए और किसी कोर्स करने की जरूरत नहीं पड़ेगी कोर्स में जिस बेस के ऊपर स्टॉक मार्केट चलती है उसको पूर्ण रूप से समझाया गया है जैसे एक विदेशी निवेशक किसी भी कंट्री में निवेश करने के लिए रिसर्च करता है उस प्रकार के नॉलेज इस कोर्स में है और फंडामेंटल के साथ-साथ टेक्निकल का भी मेल बहुत अच्छा किया गया है इसलिए कोर्स सबको करना चाहिए यह कोर्स करने के बाद आपको मार्केट के गिरावट और तेजी से किसी प्रकार का कोई डर नहीं लगेगा

Name: Jignesh B. Karkar

City: Vadodara, Gujarat

Profession: Manager – Netafim Irrigation India Pvt. Ltd., Vadodara

Since last 5 Year I continuous watching Piyush Sir's Video about Wealth Management on You Tube, I Also completed 2 Technical Work Shop, But Still Eagar to Lear More as i believing in long term wealth creation, hence in this course I learned lot, Thanks Piyush sir & Team for Their Support, In future collectively we will do better to spread financial literacy in society. Thank Lot!

Name: Deepak Wankhede

City: Surat, Gujarat

Profession: Service in Oil and Natural Gas Corporation Ltd. as General Manager (Production)

The four months course of fundamental and technical analysis was very effective and therefore I highly recommend. Piyush Patel Sir is very knowledgeable and provided a wealth of information about wealth creation through investing in stock market. Also, very supportive team of Profitfromit. Thanks.

Name: Minesh Patel

City: Jaipur

Profession: Jewelry Business

Thank you for giving me a chance to become a member of this and I got knowledge about technical and fundamental. Now I am also able to trade properly and now I am able to see the stock selection stop loss also in a good way. Thank you very much.

Name: Manjunath Rajanna

City: Bengaluru

Profession: Sales Co-Ordinator (Carrier Air Conditioner)

Amazing course. with Piyush sir teaching and guidance the stock fundamental analysis looks so easy to learn. I would suggest my friend to join if anyone is interested in learning about stock market analysis.

Student Name: Mansukhlal R. Kamani

City: Rajkot, Gujarat State

Batch: January 2022

Fundamental & technical analysis practical training program is designed very nicely. presentation & teaching method of shri. piyush sir is very simple & effectively. piyush sir is given equal weightage to all students. i am very thankful to piyush sir & profit from it team to open path of wealth creation. eventhough i have not attended properly all episodes & homework practice at satisfactory level due to my physical problem, i learned some things better for me. i once again thankful to all members of profit from it.

Name: Ashok Sonagra

City: Upleta-Rajkot (Gujarat)

I have a great learning from this online 4-month technical and fundamental course. This course helps me to understand not only the Indian stock market but also the world market. I get to know what is the importance of economic data on the future industries growth and how it is helpful to select the right sector and right stock. I've learned so many important parameters on every quarterly result exercise. Thanks to Piyush sir for giving me this opportunity

Name: Dr. Mahesh Karandikar

City: Pune

Profession: Doctor

A wonderful course taught for beginners taught very scientifically and in a very simple and lucid way by Piyush sir. Recommended to one and all interested. All the staff is also very co-operative and helpful

Name: Amarnath Thakor

City: Mahmedabad

Profession: Trainer

Profit from it is a one of the best stock market trading institute in India and change the mindset about investment.

Name Kishore Suvarna

City: Mumbai

Profession: Financial Advisor

It's by far the most reliable, honest, trustworthy and value for money course. Rather more than value for money. I promise you won't regret your investment.

Name Rakesh Gupta

City: Ghaziabad

Profession: Retired Bank Executive

Great experience, unique methodology, useful contents, makes you self-dependent in stock selection/investing. You will only invest in quality companies after course. No garbage in portfolio. Piyushbhai is very knowledgeable, Profit team is very helpful. Used to see videos on YouTube. Got impressed and joined course

Name Mukesh

City: Vadodara

Profession: Job

I was into almost 18 years into market when I took up the course "5 steps towards wealth creation". This course has brought in immense faith in Piyush bhai's teaching and boosted my confidence to sky that now onwards there won't be any loss in share market...its a life long healthy wealth creation...

Name: Dr. Milind Bidve

City: Pune

Profession: Docter

It's best training program in India .Every investor must attain 5 step of wealth creation for better investing decisions and wealth creations

www.ingramcontent.com/pod-product-compliance
Lightning Source LLC
Chambersburg PA
CBHW031552150726
47990CB00001B/318